Albert de Groot

Record of the Proceedings and Ceremonies Pertaining to the Erection of the Franklin Statue in Printing-House Square

Albert de Groot

Record of the Proceedings and Ceremonies Pertaining to the Erection of the Franklin Statue in Printing-House Square

ISBN/EAN: 9783337252724

Printed in Europe, USA, Canada, Australia, Japan

Cover: Foto ©ninafisch / pixelio.de

More available books at **www.hansebooks.com**

The Franklin Statue.

Photographed by Warren, 381 Canal St., N. Y.

PROCEEDINGS AND CEREMONIES PERTAINING
TO THE ERECTION OF

THE FRANKLIN STATUE

IN PRINTING-HOUSE SQUARE.

Presented by

ALBERT DE GROOT,

TO THE PRESS AND PRINTERS OF THE CITY OF NEW-YORK.

NEW-YORK
FRANCIS HART & CO., 12 AND 14 COLLEGE PLACE
1872.

Contents.

I.	Preface, . .	9
II.	Introduction,	11
III.	Preliminary Arrangements, .	17
IV.	Laying the Corner Stone,	25
V.	The Private View,	29
VI.	Committee Meetings,	34
VII.	Unveiling Ceremonies, .	41
VIII.	The Banquet,	51
IX.	The Comments of the Press,	83
X.	Appendix,	97

Preface.

THE Committee to whom was intrusted the collection of a fund to defray the expenses incidental to the proper reception of the generous gift of ALBERT DE GROOT, were urged by many contributors to put into permanent form an account of the entire proceedings. And believing that all who participated in the ceremonies would be glad to preserve the speeches, etc., the Committee decided to prepare and print a detailed record of all matters connected with the Statue from its inception to the close of the celebration on Franklin's Birth-day. In this they have been especially aided by Mr. T. L. De Vinne, whose firm have presented the work in their usual excellent style of typography.

Introduction.

THE succeeding pages, that are intended to describe all the details connected with the inauguration of a Statue of Franklin in our city, might safely be left to explain themselves. But, perhaps, a few additional words may appropriately introduce the subject matter which follows.

The very general and generous interest manifested in this memorial statue, furnishes reasons for believing that many more of our country's benefactors may be honored in like manner; and the detailed proceedings herein given may tend to encourage others to put in execution projects leading to similar results. The ideas advanced by some of the speakers at the Banquet—looking to the embellishment of our city by statues of eminent Americans who have deserved well of their countrymen—will, no doubt, be stimulated by the generous action of Captain De Groot.

In all such enterprises, some one individual, or a few at most, must go forward at first and assume direction, and take responsibilities, or success can never be assured. And in this particular, the following pages show just how this work was done, and how other public monuments or memorials may be secured.

Of the Statue itself, as a successful work of art, it may not be incumbent upon the Committee to speak. The criticisms, as printed, are generally very flattering to the sculptor, and it may safely be said that the Statue, as it stands to-day in its appropriate place, commands general approval. It seems to meet the popular idea of what Franklin was in form and feature; and the face is accepted as portraying, with uncommon accuracy, the noblest characteristics of the man, whose memory next to that of Washington, is most deeply set in the hearts of the American people.

But there are no works of art which escape adverse criticism. Unanimity in these matters is impossible, and perhaps undesirable; for without contrariety of opinion there could be little progress or improvement. Besides, perfection in matters of art can never be expected. No two critics can exactly agree in respect to the merits of the best artistic work yet made, and probably there never will be a human work which will be universally esteemed as entirely faultless.

No public enterprise was ever more generously commended than this. The spirit and enthusiasm of the generous donor was shared by all who aided in the various steps leading to the unveiling. And when at last the drapery was drawn from the Statue by the venerable man who so fittingly performed this act, the assembled thousands who stood awaiting to see if the figure was indeed worthy of the subject, and determined to do no honor to a work which did not fill their ideal of Franklin — when at last the Statue stood uncovered before them, one united, universal cheer broke forth, and proclaimed that the sculptor had won his triumph, and honestly earned the "well done" of the admiring multitude.

A most notable feature of the entire record, as here given, is the fact that everything was carried forward without the aid or intervention of the local government. No contribution was sought from the city corporation; permission only was asked that the Statue might stand in the public place it occupies.

It is seldom that so important and costly a work is undertaken by a private individual. Usually, the aid of associations or of the government has to be secured before a public work of art can be erected. In other countries, especially, the public monuments are almost entirely due to the action of government. But it is more in harmony with the spirit of our institutions to encourage private individuals to undertake such enterprises; and it is gratifying to know that such an ambition is developing itself in our midst. The hope expressed by Captain De Groot in his modest speech at the Banquet, will no doubt be realized, and many other memorials of our great and good men will ere long grace the public places of our land.

Much might here be said of the propriety of thus honoring the name of Franklin, and of the fitness of the memorial as a city monument in the exact place where it stands; of the grand suggestions which such a history as Franklin evokes; of its influence in keeping active and warm a spirit of patriotism; of the incentives which the humble and aspiring may receive from such a character made more definite in enduring bronze; and of the hope and encouragement which may enter the hearts of the struggling and despairing when looking upon the face of one whose biography is so full of trials and of triumphs. But all these thoughts are so fully presented in the speeches and in the editorials of the Press, that we need not enlarge upon them here.

III

Preliminary Arrangements.

WHEN the first model for the Statue had been completed, Captain De Groot invited frank criticism of the work. The model was placed in the counting-room of Messrs. Baker & Godwin, who, from the beginning of the enterprise, lost no opportunity to speed the labors of the sculptor to a successful conclusion. On the 7th May, 1870, the annexed invitation was sent to the printers and publishers of New York and Brooklyn.

Dear Sir:

Please specially oblige us by calling, on Monday or Tuesday (any hour from nine to five), at our counting-room, to see Captain Albert De Groot's idea of a colossal Statue of Franklin.

Captain De Groot intends to complete a Statue of Franklin in bronze (the model is now ready), and present it to the press and printers of New York, in testimony of his gratitude for the kindness he has received from the press, for so many years, in all the various positions he has filled.

It is proposed, by the aid of a Committee of the Press, to place this Statue of Franklin in Printing-House Square, upon a proper pedestal, with suitable railing, &c., and we hope you will favor us with a visit, and express your views respecting the model now shown in our counting-room.

Very respectfully,

Baker & Godwin.

The responses to this invitation were quite as numerous as could have been expected. The freedom of criticism that had been invited was as freely indulged. It is gratifying to note, even at this stage of the work, when the design was imperfect, that these criticisms were sympathetic and appreciative, as may be gleaned from the following extracts.

CRITICISMS ON THE SMALL MODEL.

[From the New York Times, May 10, 1870.]

So far as can be judged from the model, the attitude and expression of the figure are natural and good. Franklin is represented as wearing a plain citizen's dress. With left foot advanced, head raised, and holding a roll of papers in his left hand, he appears to be about to address some public assemblage. The model is rather too small to enable one to form a fair idea of anything more than the attitude and expression.

[From the New York World, May 10, 1870.]

The *pose* of the figure is more natural and dignified than in either the statue in Boston or that in Philadelphia, and the face is more expressive of what Franklin's character was than in either of the statues alluded to; in the former of which it wears a silly smirk, while in the latter the mouth seems to belong to a man whose chief characteristic is an imbecile desire to be benevolent to the whole universe. In Captain De Groot's statue, the face is the face of a man who, when occasion required, could not only write "Poor Richard," but could ably represent our government in a foreign court, and engage in philosophical and scientific pursuits, showing equal ability in all.

[From the Commercial Advertiser, May 11, 1870.]

It is the finest of the kind we have seen. The attitude is lofty, and the countenance noble and generous.

[From the New York Herald, May 10, 1870.]

A model for a Statue of Franklin, by Captain De Groot, exhibited yesterday in the office of Messrs. Baker & Godwin, was critically examined by a large number of newspaper men. The model is in wax, and is decidedly one of the most admirable representations of Ben Franklin that has ever yet been designed. After a careful examination of the model, the only fault which an artistic eye could discover was in the right arm, which lies too formal and straight to the body to look natural. This can be easily remedied, and then the critics will have no fault to find with the design of the artist. The intention is to complete a Statue of Franklin in bronze, and present it to the press and printers of New York. It is proposed to place the statue in Printing-House Square, upon a proper pedestal, with suitable railing, and make it an ornament and an honor to the city.

[From the New York Sun, May 11, 1870.]

We have examined the model of this Statue, and found it in every way satisfactory. The great philosopher and journalist appears in it in the costume of his time, bareheaded, with the right hand extended, as if addressing the public, and with a copy of a newspaper in the left. The design is remarkable for fidelity to the character of its distinguished subject, for dignity of mien, and impressiveness of action. A more appropriate and more munificent acknowledgment of the cordial relations which have so long existed between Captain De Groot and the newspaper press could scarcely be imagined.

[From the New York Courier, May 15, 1870.]

We have examined the model, and pronounce it as near faultless as can be. The likeness is an admirable one, and all the details of costume are perfectly reproduced. The position of the figure is easy, graceful, and at the same time eminently characteristic.

[From the New York Dispatch, May 15, 1870.]

It is the best conceived design for a Statue of "Poor Richard" that we have ever seen, and we doubt not its completion in colossal bronze will be worthy alike of the artist and his friends of the press.

Of the verbal criticisms that the model received, it is impossible to present any record; but the extracts here given may be accepted as a fair example. Careful note was taken of every suggestion for improvement and of every intimation of defect. The model was remanded to the studio, and the work of alteration and improvement was renewed.

On the 1st November, 1870, the larger model was completed, and Messrs. Baker & Godwin issued another invitation.

Dear Sir:

We trust you can make it convenient to call, between the hours of nine and eleven, any morning this week, or till November 9th, at No. 93 Sixth avenue, top floor, to see Captain De Groot's colossal Statue of Franklin (to be placed in Printing-House Square), which is now ready for casting in bronze.

Captain De Groot would esteem it a great favor if you would call as above. He will be present, and desires us to urge you to see the Statue. We think you will be repaid for the trouble.

Very respectfully,

BAKER & GODWIN.

CRITICISMS ON THE LARGE MODEL.

When the model was shown in its full proportions, and the ideal of the sculptor was more clearly developed, the merit of the work and the value of the gift were better appreciated. Journals that had contented themselves by the expression of words of polite sympathy for the motives that had prompted the designer, now freely gave hearty praise to the work itself.

[From the New York Times, November 6, 1870.]

The Statue of Franklin, intended by the generous sculptor as a free gift to the city, approaches its artistic completion. Its modeling is nearly finished, and the mechanical work to succeed is that which is of least importance. The work, as it stands, does honor to the creator of the great Vanderbilt bronze. When all the circumstances of its production are considered, we can hardly award to Captain De Groot too much credit. His work is to him indeed a labor of love, and there are traces of the fact in every stroke of his chisel. The "Franklin" is worthy of the original, and of the sculptor's fame. It is massive, simple, and yet replete with touches of artistic meaning. The subtlety that elaborated the great bronze into a thousand suggestive details, has not been lacking to give character and meaning to the counterfeit presentment of "Poor Richard." In attitude, proportions, and adjuncts, the Statue deserves peculiar study and liberal applause; and when we remember that it is to stand permanently in Printing-House Square, we cannot be too grateful to the artist who presents us with so fitting an object of contemplation. Captain De Groot deserves to be warmly congratulated on the felicitous execution of his conception, and the city upon the addition of another artistic ornament to a quarter never too rich in such desiderata. We trust the "Franklin" may long stand to commemorate the virtues and public services of the sage it represents, and the genius and liberality of the sculptor.

[From the New York Sun, November 4, 1870.]

It is an imposing figure, and was admired by those who beheld it.

[From the New York Evening Express, November 3, 1870.]

Captain De Groot, after his great success in the Vanderbilt bronzes, and in the success of an art which he has had a taste for from childhood, recently turned his attention to a Statue of Franklin, which has just been completed in plaster. It is of colossal size, and represents Franklin as he appeared at Versailles as the Ambassador of the United States. Franklin was then past seventy years, weighed 202 pounds, and stood six feet and two inches. His figure was, of course, a huge one in itself. The plaster statue is twelve feet high, and will be placed on a pedestal of the same height. The likeness to the original secured by Captain De Groot seems to us wonderfully correct, and the whole outline of form, figure, and dress, in general and in detail, gives promise of a most gratifying result when the work is put in bronze, which, we learn, will be the case during the winter, in order that the bronze Statue may be placed in Printing-House Square in the spring. The work is the free-will offering of Captain De Groot to the printers of the city, and, as such, will be gratefully appreciated by them. It is right that one almost the founder in America of "the art preservative of all arts," should be thus honored in the chief city of the country.

[From the New York Evening Post, November 3, 1870.]

The countenance is calm, reflective, and expressive, and everything about the figure is impressive. It is a success, as far as the work of the artist is concerned, and is so pronounced by competent critics.

[From the New York Dispatch, November 13, 1870.]

We are glad to note the completion, in clay, of Albert De Groot's colossal Statue of Franklin, which is to be cast in bronze and placed in Printing-House Square—a testimonial at once of the genius and liberality of its author, who makes such a princely gift to his friends, the journalists of New York. A visit to the atelier last week enables us to speak intelligently of this Statue, as a work of art; and we rejoice in the opportunity to congratulate Captain De Groot on the full success which rewards his skill and labor in the execution of a lofty and very original design. An admiring group surrounded the effigy of the "great commoner," and seemed to feel, as we did, the noble simplicity of the artist's conception, and the grand *repose* of the figure that impresses us at its first view. Such, indeed, might have been the attitude of Franklin, the American ambassador, majestic in his republican independence, before the courtiers of Versailles, or as he stood in that historic interview with the Lords in Council, at Whitehall, London, in 1774, so graphically delineated by the painter Schuessele.

There is about the Statue a marvelous ease, so to speak, which, at the same time, does not detract from the sturdy *pose* of the lower limbs, sustaining the well-poised *torso*, the gracefully-inclined head, and "Poor Richard's" familiar face looking down, with kindly wisdom. The idea and accomplishment of this massive model furnish the best answer that could be given to the cavils and scepticisms of those who assume to pass judgment on American ability to excel in the plastic art; denying our sculptors the incentives to true ambition, by persisting in a flippant denial of American claims and a fulsome adulation of foreign pretensions.

Captain De Groot, it is fortunate, lacks not the means to substantiate American claims, by executing his rare artistic conceptions without being compelled to await the tardy appreciation of patronizing *connoisseurs*; and the result is, that he produces a Statue which challenges comparison with both native and foreign achievements in modeling. We feel confident that the verdict of both critics and the public will be given in approval of this work, and that the untiring genius of our American artist, Albert De Groot, will be rewarded by "golden opinions" from the press, in whose honor the Statue of Franklin is to be raised, in colossal bronze, on Printing-House Square.

While the work of founding the Statue was in progress, active measures were taken by Mr. Baker to enlist the sympathies of the printers and publishers of New York in the work. To secure their coöperation in the contribution of a fitting pedestal, was the occasion of the following circular.

THE FRANKLIN STATUE.

As is quite generally known, Captain Albert De Groot has been for some time engaged in casting a colossal Statue of Franklin in bronze. It will be completed within three months, and ready to place in Printing-House Square during September, 1871. The permission of the city authorities has already been obtained.

Captain De Groot exhibited the model, in plaster, at Plassman's School of Art (Sixth avenue), for several weeks; and a very large number of gentlemen connected with the press, as well as sculptors and artists, inspected the model; and nearly all pronounced the Statue worthy of the subject, creditable to the designer, and every way fit to rank with the best public monuments.

Captain De Groot generously contributes the bronze Statue—which is estimated to cost over $15,000—to the press of New York, as a free-will testimonial of his respect for the character of Franklin, and as a return for the kindness always bestowed upon him by the press of this city.

It is now proposed to form a committee from the members of the newspaper and periodical press, to provide for the construction of a proper pedestal, railing, &c., and to make the necessary arrangements for the inauguration ceremonies.

The sum of five thousand dollars is thought to be needed for a proper granite pedestal, railing, &c., and toward the raising of this sum you are respectfully asked to contribute.

Mr. Samuel Sinclair, the publisher of the New York Tribune, has consented to act as treasurer of the fund, to whose order checks may be made payable.

IV

Laying the Corner-Stone.

ON the 2d October, 1871, the ground in Printing-House Square was broken for the reception of the corner-stone. In deference to established usage, and the expressed desire of many interested, Mr. Daniel Godwin was commissioned, on behalf of the press of the city, to invite the Hon. John H. Anthon, M. W. G. M. of the Masonic fraternity of the State of New York, to lay the corner-stone, with proper Masonic ceremonies. This invitation was accepted, and the annexed circular was issued.

Dear Sir:

The corner-stone of the Franklin Statue in Printing-House Square will be laid with Masonic ceremonies, by M. W. John H. Anthon, Grand Master of Masons of the State of New York, on Thursday, October 26, at one o'clock P. M.

You are cordially invited to be present on that occasion.

Respectfully yours,
On behalf of the Committee,

BAKER & GODWIN.

NEW YORK, October [illegible], 1871.

The corner-stone for the pedestal and Statue of Benjamin Franklin was accordingly laid, with Masonic ceremonies, at two o'clock, October 26, 1871.

Notwithstanding the drizzling rain which prevailed, a large number of persons collected to witness the ceremony. The Fifth

Regiment Band was stationed within the railing, and performed selections of music prior to the ceremony.

There were present Captain De Groot, Mr. Peter Cooper, and John H. Anthon, Grand Master; Right Worshipful E. P. Breed, D. G. M.; E. L. Judson, S. G. W.; James L. Husted, J. G. W.; John W. Simons, Grand Treasurer; James M. Austin, Grand Secretary; W. R. Brown, S. G. D.; Enoch George, J. G. D.; Isaac H. Brown, Grand Steward; O. G. Brady, Steward; R. L. Schoonmaker, Grand Chaplain; Charles W. Roome, Grand Marshal; John Hoole, Grand Tiler; Johnston Fountain, Grand Pursuivant; District Deputies E. E. Thorne, John A. Foster, H. W. Turner, C. B. Wade, and Charles Sackreuter.

Having been arranged about the foundation of the monument, the members seated themselves upon settees, and Colonel Edward L. Gaul, of the New York Times, on behalf of the committee, introduced the Grand Master, with the following remarks:

The occasion which calls us together to-day is well known to the greater number of those here present, but for the benefit of those who are in ignorance, it may be well to state, that upon this foundation, the corner-stone of which is about to be laid, is to be erected a colossal Statue of Benjamin Franklin, which, through the liberality of a well-known citizen of the metropolis (Captain De Groot) is, when completed, to be dedicated to the press and the printers of New York. To the press this honor is rather an unusual one; for silent laborers, as its servants are, instead of being rewarded, are rather accustomed to see others reaping the results of their work. In the gift itself there is a peculiar appropriateness, for the monument is in honor of an old printer, and one whose memory to the craft is ever green. The site chosen for its location is also a fitting one, for, surrounded as it is by the great newspaper offices of the period—offices which each day gather, print, and send forth to this Western hemisphere the news of the world—we can almost feel that should the spirit of Franklin visit the bronze erected in his honor, Poor Richard would feel at home again, and among the familiar scenes of his youth.

At this time, however, any but a brief speech would be out of place, and therefore I shall only say that those having this work in charge felt that it should be properly begun, and, as is customary on occasions like this, desired that the corner-stone should be laid under the auspices of the ancient and honorable fraternity of Freemasons. I, therefore, in the name of the committee, do now invite you, John H. Anthon, Most Worshipful Grand Master of Masons of this State, to proceed with the customary ceremonies.

Grand Master Anthon replied, that Free and Accepted Masons were ever willing to assist in labors which were in consonance with their principles; and he therefore accepted the invitation, and was here to perform this duty. But Masons never began any work without invoking thereon the blessing of the Great Architect: therefore, he called upon the Right Worshipful and Reverend Mr. Schoonmaker, Grand Chaplain, to do so.

Then followed the prayer, and the reading of the contents of the box placed in the corner-stone. The box contained:

1. Constitution of the United States.
2. Constitution of the State of New York.
3. Manual of the State of New York.
4. Corporation Manual of the City of New York.
5. Parton's Life of Franklin.
6. Copy of the Holy Scriptures.
7. Map of New York City.
8. Appleton's Railway Guide.
9. Hoe's Catalogue of Printing Machines, etc.
10. Type Founders' Specimen Books.
11. Almanacs, Calendars, and Business Cards of New York Printers.
12. New York City Newspapers.
13. Illustrated Papers and Map of Chicago, describing the recent conflagration.

The square was then applied to the stone by Enoch P. Breed, Deputy Grand Master; the level, by E. R. Judson, Senior Grand Warden; and the plumb by James W. Husted, Junior Grand

Warden. They reported that the work had been properly performed, and the stone was then lowered into its place. Corn, wine, and oil were then poured upon it. Grand Marshal Charles Roome then declared the corner-stone to be properly laid according to the rules of Masonry; the Grand Master pronounced the ceremony completed; and, after assembling his brother officers, marched out of the enclosure. The assemblage then dispersed.

V

The Private View.

WHEN the casting of the Statue had been completed, the press and the artists of the city were again invited. It was believed that the close inspection which the Statue would receive in the foundry, accompanied as it would be by the personal explanations of the artist and founder, would enable every thoughtful observer to form a better conception of the value of the gift and of the merit of the work. With this object in view, the annexed circular was issued.

Dear Sir:

You are respectfully invited to a private view of the Franklin Statue to be presented, by Albert De Groot, to the press and printers of New York, on Tuesday, December 5, 1871, at the foundry of Fischer Brothers, No. 209 Forsyth street, near Houston street, rear building.

The Statue is now completed; we believe it will please you; and we earnestly ask for your presence between the hours of twelve and two, on Tuesday, as above named.

Very respectfully,

BAKER & GODWIN.

NEW YORK, December 2, 1871

This invitation brought together a large number of journalists, printers, and publishers, and some artists. It was known that the casting was one of the largest ever made in this country, and there was much curiosity on the part of all interested in founding or statuary to ascertain how the mechanical as well as the artistic difficulties had been treated. Like all other statues, it received its share of complimentary and of disparaging criticism; but the opinion of those who by education and pursuits were best qualified to judge impartially was that of warm commendation. As the Statue was of colossal size, nearly twelve feet high, and made to be seen by observers at a distance, who from the ground should look upward, this close inspection at the private view was not calculated to produce the best impression. But this proximity gave good opportunity for an examination of the careful mechanical finish, which was generally approved.

It was stated that the bronze used in the Statue was of superior quality, even for statuary. An unusual proportion of the metal is pure copper. The weight of the Statue was estimated at 3,500 pounds, and its value, when completed, at $15,000. The pedestal and its appurtenances, with the surrounding railing and lamps, were estimated to be of the value of $5,000.

The extracts from the journals, which are appended, will fairly represent the opinions of most of the critics then present.

[From the New York Standard December 6, 1871.]

Captain De Groot and Mr. Plassman have produced what we must deem a perfect success. Of the effect, when placed on its pedestal, we can only imagine. As it stands now, the *pose* is admirable. One hand is stretched forth, as if in speaking; the other holds a copy of "The Pennsylvanian," his first paper. The natural relaxation of the muscles, which yet hold the folds in easy grasp, is most admirable. The dress is copied accurately from the pictures of Franklin—ruffles, knee-breeches, and all. The long-waisted coat and ample vest give something of a stunted appearance to the legs; yet this apparent defect is essential to our idea of the man, and quite supersedes the desire for more artistic proportions. The view from the rear is very striking. There would be no mistaking the breadth of back, the slightly stooping shoulders, and flowing hair. The face is the result of the comparison of the best pictures of Franklin and a bust in Philadelphia. When we say it returns to us our own conception of the merry-hearted philosopher, whose far-searching eyes pierced the deep and profound, and chained the fateful lightning, while the genial smile hovered about the mouth of the sage, who did not disdain to extract all the cheer possible from this world's goods, notwithstanding his economical maxims: can we say more?

[From the New York Evening Express, December 5, 1871.]

The face of Franklin seems to us to be perfect; certainly it is in full accord with the best likenesses handed down from his own time. The workmanship upon the features and dress shows great skill, taste, and perfection, and leaves nothing to be desired.

[From the New York Sun, December 6, 1871.]

The old philosopher and statesman is represented in the dress he wore at Versailles—large lappel coat, a long vest to match, knee-breeches, ruffled shirt-front and cuffs, and shoes with broad buckles. The figure is bare-headed, with long flowing hair, and the likeness is decidedly striking and effective.

[From the New York Observer, December 14, 1871.]

De Groot's Statue of Franklin, to stand in Printing-House Square in this city, is a great success. The likeness to the traditional portraits of the philosopher is wonderful, and the figure is admirable.

THE PEDESTAL.

At this meeting was also submitted the designs for the pedestal, which may here be more fully described.

The granite was taken from the quarry at Mill-Stone Point, about six miles from New London, Connecticut.

The lower base is the largest block of granite that has ever been produced from this quarry, which has been worked for more than fifty years. In its rough state it weighed nearly sixteen tons, and is about the largest single piece of granite that has ever been drawn over the Broadway pavement, being eight feet six inches square and two feet ten inches thick. The second base is composed of two blocks of granite. The upper base is moulded. The die is composed of a single block of granite, being five feet high and four feet four inches square. The cap, upon which the Statue rests, is also composed of one single block, being four feet nine inches square and one foot seven inches thick.

The entire pedestal is all fine-hammered. The constructors consider themselves fortunate in getting the various blocks of such large dimensions free from flaws and defects.

The foundation upon which the pedestal rests was built eight feet six inches square, and seven feet below the surface of the street, of large blocks of building stones, laid in the best quality of cement. The pedestal, in its proportions, is of the modern style of architecture.

This pedestal was constructed by Fisher & Bird, of Houston street, New York, and is highly praised by critics for the simplicity of its design, its careful workmanship, and the pleasing effect of its proportions.

The work on the pedestal and the lamps and railing was completed on the 6th January. On Wednesday, the 10th January, the Statue was erected on its pedestal, and enveloped in the drapery of the American flag, in which state it remained until unveiled, on Franklin's birthday.

At a subsequent meeting it was definitely agreed that the arrangements for the reception of the Statue, and the ceremonies connected therewith, should be entrusted to a special committee, that should fairly represent every one of the many interests connected with typography. With this understanding, the annexed circular was issued.

Dear Sir:

You are probably familiar with the fact that Albert De Groot has, at his own expense, completed a colossal bronze Statue of Franklin (modeled and sculptured by Ernst Plassman, cast by George Fischer & Brother), to be presented to the press and printers of New York.

It is now proposed to appoint a committee, representing our profession, to formally receive this generous gift of Captain De Groot, and to make suitable arrangements for the unveiling of the Statue on Franklin's birthday, in Printing-House Square.

As it is designed to make the occasion one of general interest to the press and printers of New York, you are specially requested to be present at a meeting to be held at the Astor House (room 14), on Thursday afternoon, January 4, 1872, at three o'clock.

At this meeting a committee will be appointed to make all the necessary arrangements connected with the unveiling of the Statue, and for the appropriate celebration of Franklin's birthday, on the 17th of January.

We trust you may feel a personal interest in this matter, and not fail to be present at the time and place above named.

Very respectfully,

BAKER & GODWIN,	ERASTUS BROOKS,
GEORGE JONES,	JOSEPH ELLIOTT,
SAMUEL SINCLAIR,	D. D. T. MOORE,
THOS. N. ROOKER,	N. D. BANGS,
OSWALD OTTENDORFER,	J. M. BUNDY,
THEO. L. DE VINNE,	EDWARD O. JENKINS.
ISAAC W. ENGLAND,	

NEW YORK, January 2, 1872.

VI

Committee Meetings.

IN response to the previous notice, a large number of journalists and printers met at the Astor House on the 4th day of January, 1872, for the purpose of making suitable arrangements for the unveiling of the Statue, and for devising such measures as would insure the appropriate celebration of Franklin's birthday. Rev. Dr. S. Irenæus Prime was called to the Chair, and Peter C. Baker was appointed Secretary.

Rev. Dr. Prime, as Chairman of the meeting, secured order, and directed its action. After a reading of the circular, Mr. Baker explained the history of the Statue, and suggested that some action be taken in reference to the pedestal, which cost $3,600, and "is to be paid for by the press and printers."

The following named gentlemen were constituted a Committee on Finance:

SAMUEL SINCLAIR, H. C. BOWEN, GEORGE JONES,
THEO. L. DE VINNE, PETER C. BAKER.

A Committee of Arrangements was appointed, with power to make an order of exercises for the ceremonies at the reception of the Statue, and for the celebration of Franklin's Birthday on the same evening. A general desire was manifested for a commemoration in the nature of a social entertainment. The committee were therefore authorized to make preparations for a banquet suitable for the occasion.

The following named gentlemen were duly constituted as the Committee of Arrangements:

Douglas Taylor,	James L. Smith,	Fletcher Harper, Jr.,
Erastus Brooks,	Sinclair Tousey,	Thomas N. Rooker,
I. W. England,	Daniel Godwin,	John F. Baldwin.
N. D. Bangs,	Joseph Howard, Jr.,	

The following named gentlemen were nominated and elected as members of the General Committee:

Jas. Gordon Bennett,	Henry Ward Beecher,	John Harper,
Horace Greeley,	S. M. Isaacs,	C. H. Williams,
Wm. C. Bryant,	George R. Crooks,	Fletcher Harper, Jr.,
George Jones,	H. W. Bellows,	J. B. Ford,
Charles A. Dana,	Robert M. De Witt,	A. S. Barnes,
Manton Marble,	James Glastaeter,	Chas. C. Savage,
Erastus Brooks,	Richard B. Kimball,	John Dougall,
D. M. Stone	Henry M. Field,	James Parton,
William C. Prime,	J. Cotton Smith,	S. Irenæus Prime,
J. Russell Young,	Thomas N. Rooker,	Sidney E. Morse,
Oswald Ottendorfer,	Joseph Elliott,	Peter S. Hoe,
J. G. Bennett, Jr.,	D. D. T. Moore,	C. A. Alvord,
J. M. Bundy,	James L. Smith,	Peter C. Baker,
Hugh J. Hastings,	M. F. Gale,	Samuel Orchard,
Geo. Wilkes,	E. G. Howard,	J. S. Du Solle,
James White,	H. C. Watson,	Wm B. Dana,
Theo. L. De Vinne,	Orange Judd,	Edwin A. Elcock,
E. O. Jenkins,	Jno. G. Lightbody,	Edward Bright,
Daniel Godwin,	Sheldon Collins,	Piercey Wilson,
Benjamin Wood,	Theodore Tilton,	George Roberts,
A. J. H. Duganne,	Orson B. Munn,	J. H. Van Evrie,
J. A. McMasters,	M. M. Pomeroy,	J. Bondi,
Joseph Howard, Jr.,	Sinclair Tousey,	Nicoll Floyd,
Fletcher Harper,	Isaac Henderson,	H. D. Wade,
Wm. H. Appleton,	N. D. Bangs,	Alfred E. Beach,
Geo. P. Putnam,	Isaac W. England,	Henry Dexter,
Peter Carter,	Geo. F. Nesbitt,	S. H. Wales,
Henry Ivison,	Wm. Cauldwell,	Francis S. Smith,
Geo. W. Carleton	Francis S. Street,	William Brown,
J. S. Redfield,	W. C. Church,	William B. Bogge,
Wm. A. Townsend,	H. C. Page,	Robert McKechnie,
Robert Bonner,	E. D. Holmes,	J. H. Goodsell,

Samuel Sinclair,
Robert Hoe,
E. L. Godkin,
Alex. Campbell,
A. B. Taylor,
Wm. C. Martin,
John F. Trow,
David W. Bruce,
Wm. C. Conner,
A. D. Farmer,
Andrew Little,
Wm. Hagar,
Geo. P. Rowell,
S. M. Pettengill,
W. W. Sharpe,
Douglas Taylor,
H. C. Bowen,
Frank Leslie,
Geo. W Curtis,
E. G. Squier,
Edward G. Prime,
C. Van Wyck,
James Sutton,
George Munro,
A. D. F. Randolph,
M. B. Wynkoop,
Feodore Mierson,
Thomas Carlton,
C. M. Herrick,
F. Rauchfuss,
Chas. La Salle,
R. B. Roosevelt,
Geo. W. Matsell,
Frank Queen,
Cornelius Mathews,
S. P. Dinsmore,
Thos. H. Senior,
Lewis Francis,
John W. Oliver,
George P. Gordon,
Francis Hart,
John Mullaly,
George Dexter,
John F. Baldwin,
Solomon L. Cohen,
M. B. Brown,
Ralph N. Perlee,
Samuel Booth,
John Medole,
James Powers,
E. S. Dodge,
S. W. Green,
Chas. McDevitt,
Samuel French,
M. K. Pelletreau,
J. F. Knapp,
John Polhemus,
Joseph Russell,
J. H. Hallenbeck,
George McDougal,
E. D. Slater,
Thomas C. Faulkner,
Henry W. Turner.

Peter C. Baker, Secretary. S. Irenæus Prime, Chairman.

The time for action was limited, but the committee were active, and the necessary arrangements were quickly made. To secure a general approval of their action, the committee issued the annexed circular to the trade.

Dear Sir:

At a large meeting of members of the press, publishers, and printers of the city of New York, held at the Astor House, January 4th, for the purpose of making arrangements for the appropriate celebration of Franklin's birthday (in connection with the unveiling of Franklin's Statue, in Printing-House Square), a committee was appointed to report a programme for the occasion.

You are now respectfully invited to be present at the general meeting, at the Astor House, on Tuesday afternoon, January 9th, at two o'clock, to hear the report of this committee, and to aid in securing the success of the celebration.

We earnestly desire the presence of every gentleman on the General Committee (of which you were chosen a member), and trust you will favor us with your attendance.

The time is short, but if the attendance be large, the celebration can be made entirely satisfactory, and worthy of the occasion.

We beg for your interest and presence.

PETER C. BAKER, Secretary. S. IRENÆUS PRIME, Chairman.

DOUGLAS TAYLOR,
ERASTUS BROOKS,
ISAAC W. ENGLAND,
FLETCHER HARPER, Jr.,
JOSEPH HOWARD, Jr.,
SINCLAIR TOUSEY,
DANIEL GODWIN,
N. D. BANGS,
JAS. L. SMITH,
THOS. N. ROOKER,
JOHN F. BALDWIN,

Committee of Arrangements.

NEW YORK, January 8, 1872.

This call for a meeting was equally successful in securing a large attendance of printers and publishers. The room was well filled, and much interest was manifested in the proceedings.

The Committee of Arrangements, through their chairman, Mr. Douglas Taylor, reported that the day celebration would take place at twelve o'clock, on Franklin's Birthday, when the Statue would be unveiled, presented to the press, and formally received by Mr. Charles C. Savage, on behalf of the New York Typographical Society.

The order of exercises at the unveiling would be—

1. Music by Otto's Band.
2. Prayer by Rev. Dr. Deems.
3. Unveiling of the Statue. By Professor S. B. F. Morse.
4. Presentation of the Statue to the Press and Printers of New York. (On behalf of Albert De Groot.) By Horace Greeley.
5. Acceptance of the Statue. By Charles C. Savage, President of the Board of Trustees of the New York Typographical Society.
6. Music by the Band.

The platform around the Statue would be occupied by representative members of the press, and by invited guests. The various newspaper establishments, and the employing printers of the city, were requested to give their workmen the necessary time to witness the ceremonies.

In the evening, a banquet would take place at Delmonico's, on Fourteenth street and Fifth avenue. The following gentlemen were invited to respond to the toasts: Horace Greeley, Rev. Henry Ward Beecher, Rev. Dr. Chapin, Hon. Erastus Brooks, H. O. Houghton, Rev. Mr. Duane, and his Honor A. Oakey Hall, Mayor of the city.

The price of tickets, of which but 150 were to be issued, was limited to ten dollars.

In compliance with instructions, the Committee of Arrangements issued the following invitation:

Dear Sir:

You are respectfully and earnestly invited to be present at the unveiling of the Franklin Statue, presented by Albert De Groot to the press and printers of New York city, in Printing-House Square, on Wednesday, January 17th, at twelve o'clock.

As the occasion will be one of special interest, we hope you will favor us by your presence.

Very respectfully,

Douglas Taylor,
Erastus Brooks,
Isaac W. England,
Fletcher Harper, Jr.,
Joseph Howard, Jr.,
Sinclair Tousey,
Daniel Godwin,
N. D. Bangs,
Jas. L. Smith,
Thos. N. Rooker,
John F. Baldwin,

Committee of Arrangements.

New York, January 11, 1872.

The action of the committee was approved, and the members were authorized to perfect other arrangements without further direction.

At an adjourned meeting of the Committee of Arrangements, held at the Astor House, on the 12th January, it was reported that Mr. Greeley and Professor S. B. F. Morse had accepted the duties requested of them at the unveiling of the Statue. Acceptances of invitation were also read from other gentlemen. The Rev. J. A. Spencer, S. B. F. Morse, Peter Cooper, Rev. Mr. B. Duane (a grandson of Benjamin Franklin), and others, were added to the list of invited guests. Rev. Dr. S. Irenæus Prime was selected to preside at the banquet.

A list of toasts and responses was adopted, as follows:

1. The President of the United States.
2. The State of New York and the City of New York.
3. Benjamin Franklin.
4. Honesty the Best Policy.
5. Our Friend and our Guest, Captain Albert De Groot.
6. Our Country.
7. Public Opinion.
8. The Press.
9. The Working Press.
10. Our Judges.
11. American Literature.
12. Our Mothers and our Wives; Our Daughters and our Sisters.

VII

Unveiling the Franklin Statue.

LONG before the appointed hour Printing-House Square was filled with a quiet and orderly assemblage, and the City Hall Park was crowded with spectators. The number was variously estimated at from twenty to thirty thousand. The assemblage extended across Park Row, blocking up the street and preventing travel, reaching out toward Tryon Row and the side streets. All the windows and balconies in the neighborhood were filled with ladies. The most sanguine among the projectors of the celebration could not have anticipated that it would have been witnessed by so great a concourse of people. Flags were raised on all the newspaper offices, and banners floated from the roof of the City Hall and adjacent buildings.

The weather was propitious. There had been forebodings of a snow storm; the air was keen and cold; but before noon the sun was shining brightly.

In front of the Statue a platform had been erected for the accommodation of the members of the committee and the invited guests. Another and smaller platform was assigned to Captain De Groot, Professor Morse, Horace Greeley, and Charles C. Savage.

The police arrangements were excellent, but the hundred and fifty men would have been powerless to keep the space around the Statue clear had they not been assisted by strong stakes and chains.

Soon after twelve o'clock, the Committee of Arrangements, invited guests, and representatives of the press and printers of New York, formed in order at the foot of Franklin's Statue, in Printing-House Square. With the banner and the representatives of the New York Typographical Society at the head of the line, the committee entered the enclosure and ascended the platform. Professor Morse was supported on one side by Horace Greeley and by Peter Cooper on the other.

Among those present were Benjamin Franklin Bache, a descendant of the great printer, Sinclair Tousey, Douglas Taylor, William C. Conner, Andrew Little, Thomas Acton, George P. Rowell, Henry Ivison, Henry C. Bowen, Samuel Sinclair, John F. Trow, William C. Martin, H. O. Houghton, Samuel French, Thomas N. Rooker, Charles McDevitt, C. A. Alvord, David W. Bruce, and Lewis Francis, together with a large number of old or prominent printers, journalists, and publishers, and the representatives of the municipal government. General regret was expressed that the sickness of Ernst Plassman prevented him from witnessing the unveiling of the Statue.

The Rev. Dr. Prime opened the proceedings with the following remarks:

Fellow-Citizens:

The day, too long delayed, has at length arrived: the day that beholds in the city of New York a Statue of the illustrious Franklin. Through the munificence of one of our own citizens, this splendid and fitting monument is ours; and while it stands in this Printing-House Square, it will perpetuate the genius of Franklin and the generosity of Captain De Groot. We are about to unveil this Statue in the face of Heaven, and prayer will now be offered by Rev. Dr. Deems.

The Rev. Dr. Deems, pastor of the Church of the Strangers, offered the following prayer:

Almighty God, our Heavenly Father, we adore Thee for Thy great goodness, in that Thou hast begotten the race of men to be Thy children on the earth. As Thy children, we are Thine heirs; heirs of God and joint heirs with Christ Jesus. Thou hast most kindly given us part of Thy universe to enjoy here, and hast in store for us an inheritance incorruptible, and undefiled, and never fading away.

We thank Thee, Holy Father, for all those who, going before us, have made the road of human pilgrimage more easy and the way of human duty more plain.

We thank Thee for Memory, which keeps the greatness and goodness of one generation to stimulate the following generations to greatness and goodness.

For all the good which has been wrought by the example and labors and teachings of him to whom this Statue is to-day erected, we render thanks to Thee, O blessed Lord, from whom cometh every good and perfect gift. We pray that that good influence may grow from age to age. Whatever was narrow or low, we beseech Thee to neutralize, by the power of Thy Spirit, in the hearts of men, and by the spread of the principles of the Gospel of our Lord and Saviour Jesus Christ.

Part of our sin, O Lord, is in that we have abused this present world, not using it for its highest purposes, not extracting from it its greatest and best delights. For this sin we most penitently beseech Thee to forgive us. And we pray that ever hereafter we may have wisdom and grace to use the world of matter and of mind in such a way as to draw therefrom strength and sweetness and beauty into our own souls, and to impart thereunto such a blessing that those who come after us shall find this part of our Father's domain beautified and improved by our residence.

And so, O blessed Lord, do we pray for ourselves. Strengthen in us all that is good and destroy in us all that is evil, and grant us grace so to live that if no record be made of our lives, and human art contribute nothing to the perpetuation of our memories, our names may be written in the Book of Life.

We pray that all we who are here assembled may have grace, each in his measure and place, to leave behind us the power of a pure influence, even if we may not secure the temporary splendor of an earthly fame. May we remember that the praise of men is a breath, and the fear of man is a snare, and the glory of men as the flower of the field which perisheth, and that all flesh is as grass; but that they that turn many to righteousness shall shine as the stars for ever and ever.

And now, O Thou who didst command the light to shine out of darkness, hear our prayers for the press in this country. We thank Thee that, as the ages pass by, Thou art bringing men into closer brotherhood, and hast given unto us this great engine of power. Grant unto our generation grace to use it wisely. May no man lay unholy hands thereto, but every man employ it as a consecrated instrumentality, in the use of which there is a dread responsibility. So let it be the guardian of public and private truth and honor, and the terror of all them that do wickedly.

O Prince of Peace, bless the arts of peace and cause them to flourish, and bring to nought the arts of war and the fame of warriors, until all men shall call peace-makers blessed, "the sons of God," and war-makers accursed, the children of the devil.

Above all, let the name of Jesus, our Redeemer, endure as long as the sun and moon, and all glory be given to Him, and every knee bow, and every tongue confess that Jesus Christ is Lord, to the glory of God the Father. To the universe grant this, Holy Father, and to each of us grant grace so to live that we may be numbered with Thy saints in glory everlasting.

The Chairman of the Committee of Arrangements then introduced Professor Morse, who said that he esteemed it one of his highest honors that he had been designated to perform the office of unveiling this Statue. No one had more reason to venerate Franklin than himself. He closed by expressing the hope that Franklin's illustrious example of devotion to the interests of universal humanity would be the seed of further fruit for the good of mankind.

At the request of the Committee of Arrangements, Professor Morse was induced to write out his remarks made at the unveiling. This manuscript has been faithfully reproduced by the American Photo-Lithographic Company. The copy of this manuscript, which is inserted as the opposite page, will be highly prized, not only by every printer as a specimen of a new and curious art, but by every American for its autograph of so worthy and honored a successor of Franklin.

Mr. Degroot and Fellow-citizens

I esteem it one of my highest honors that I should have been designated to perform the Office of unveiling this day the fine statue of our illustrious & immortal Franklin.

When requested to accept this duty I was confined to my bed, but I could not refuse, and I said yes if I had to be lifted to the spot. Franklin needs no eulogy from me. No one has more reason to venerate his name than myself. May his illustrious example of devotion to the interests of universal humanity be the seed of further fruit for the good of the world. —

S. F. B. Morse

The Statue was then unveiled. As the drapery fell from the figure, the "Star Spangled Banner" was played by the band, loud cheers arose from the crowd, and a salute of artillery was fired in the City Hall Park.

Immediately after the unveiling of the Statue, Mr. Morse left his position on the platform. His place was taken by Mr. Charles C. Savage, President of the Board of Trustees of the New York Typographical Society, to whom Mr. Horace Greeley, in behalf of Captain De Groot, made the following address:

PRESENTATION SPEECH BY HORACE GREELEY.

Mr. President, and Gentlemen of the Press and Typographic Profession:

A Statue of Franklin was suggested by one of our craft as appropriate to be inaugurated in this great city, which has become the emporium of American journalism and of American book-publishing. It seems to be desirable and proper that the printers and publishers of the city of New York should testify their regard for the man whom we all esteem as a patriot, a sage, and the chief honor of our calling, by presenting some visible embodiment of him to the admiration and appreciation of our fellow-citizens. This suggestion was made to Captain Albert De Groot, who, as he says, in acknowledgment of the many favors he has received from the press of this city, resolved himself to be the originator of this Statue, and thus the benefactor of our calling. Captain De Groot conferred with Mr. Ernst Plassman, a distinguished sculptor of our city, and employed him to put his idea into enduring material, which now, in his behalf, I am enabled to present to you, gentlemen of the press and of the typographic art. I rejoice that this work is, like its subject, purely American. It may be that European art is able at this stage to have produced a better one—though I think not. But, at all events, the production of this is our warrant for believing, that if better statues can be created, we have by this example—by this achievement—prepared our countrymen to produce them in a future not distant. I rejoice, fellow-citizens, that, while presenting an American Statue of an American philosopher, the gift of a public-spirited American citizen, we have been assisted in inaugurating this Statue by that eminent American discoverer who to-day is the nearest resemblance to the great and patriotic citizen whose memory we all honor. I rejoice that Professor Morse—born in that very city of Boston, within rifle-shot of Franklin's birth-place and the year after Franklin died, and who seems to have been raised up by Providence to be the continuer of that great work of which Franklin was the beginner—I rejoice that he has been spared to meet with us on this interesting occasion. This man seems to me to be the proper successor of Franklin: the one taught the world how to tame the lightning, and the other has taught us how to render it most useful as a messenger of intelligence across continents and oceans; so that to-day, by the invention of Morse, the whole world is placed in instantaneous communication, and any interesting event is flashed as by the lightning from one end of the habitable globe to the other. So I may say, fellow-citizens, in honor of Franklin, and I may also say in honor of Morse, I present, in behalf of Captain De Groot, this Statue of our great exemplar to our intelligent and, I trust, appreciative profession.

At the conclusion of Mr. Greeley's remarks, which were much applauded, Mr. Charles C. Savage, in accepting the Statue, replied as follows:

SPEECH OF ACCEPTANCE BY CHARLES C. SAVAGE.

Albert De Groot, and Gentlemen of the Press:

The agreeable duty has been assigned me to represent the New York Typographical Society on this memorable occasion, and in its name, and on behalf of the members of the press, to accept the sacred trust you to-day confide to it and them.

To be selected as the perpetual custodian of a valued treasure is an honor that any society, any body of men, would appreciate as the strongest expression of confidence which could be bestowed.

On this colossal Statue of Benjamin Franklin, the acknowledged patron saint of the printers of America, and a peer among the immortal names in history, you have concentrated your love of art, and manifested your admiration of the "Art preservative of all Arts." And now you unselfishly crown your devotion by generously donating this noble Statue to the Press and Printers of New York. On its chaste and massive pedestal, simple and beautiful in its proportions, as was the life of him whom it is designated to portray, ever may it imperishable stand. You have watched the details of the creation of this Statue in the modeling hand of the artist, Ernst Plassman, with all the zeal and thought and tenderness of a parent for his offspring. And I thank him and you, in the name of the printers of New York, that you have not departed from the real Franklin we so love to cherish, to give us an ideal hero clothed in the toga of an ancient Roman or a mythological Greek.

There he stands; embodying our idea of the printer, the philosopher, the statesman. There is the dress which Franklin wore before sages, diplomats, and kings. How vividly it recalls the suit in which he appeared at the signing of the treaty of peace with Great Britain in 1783, which, ten years before, he declared he would never wear again until he had "signed England's degradation and America's independence."

Look on that face. How full of the characteristics of the calm, sturdy, quaint common sense which marked and made Ben Franklin stand out among the intellectual giants of his day, with clear positive individuality.

Is not the whole a type of the man as he was—as we would have him be? Will it not prove a mentor and preacher to the boys and young men of this metropolis who shall gaze on the venerable form, from this text in his indenture of apprenticeship: "Taverns, inns, and ale-houses, he shall not frequent; at cards, dice, or any unlawful game, he shall not play." They will find that following his example is far better than "giving too much for the whistle" of experience, as did "Poor Richard."

It is appropriate that this Statue should be erected in this centre of our trade, in the very midst of our craft-work, instead of in Central Park; for Franklin's life was devoted to practical hard work, rather than to the ornamental and the recreative. Could Franklin step into the mammoth printing and newspaper offices which surround this monument—could he look into yonder post office—what thoughts and contrasts would they suggest! When he first visited New York, in 1723, not a newspaper was published in this city, and only one small printing office existed. And when, a few years later, he was appointed postmaster in Philadelphia, the whole mail of the country would not equal that which now passes through our city office in an hour.

But this is not the place, nor is mine the privilege, of pronouncing an eulogy on the life and works of him who is so truthfully presented in the bronze before us. Else, gladly would I recount to you his trials and successes, and the causes which led thereto; and speak of his maxims, which have almost the wisdom of inspiration. I would remind you of Franklin's habits of industry and frugality, whereby he early acquired ease in business and wealth; of his unswerving integrity, which secured him the steadfast confidence of his countrymen; of his fidelity and patriotism, which brought him the highest honors and offices in the gift of his country; of his sagacity and justice, which enabled him to cope with and master the most astute statesmen of Europe; of his studiousness and research, which gave him the key to unlock the Divine Arcana, and present to the world priceless treasures; and of his temperance, which preserved a sound mind in a healthy body for more than four-score years. In a word, Franklin was ever diligent, in whatever department he labored, to leave it better than he found it; and he stamped all with the simplicity, genius, and grandeur of his unaffected manhood. Surely, such a man is a co-worker with the Deity, to uplift humanity, and bring the race nearer to freedom, to brotherhood, and to God.

Permit me to trespass on your time to give some reasons why the Society to whom this trust is confided is worthy of the responsibility.

The New York Typographical Society is one of the oldest institutions of printers in the United States. It was organized in 1809, and incorporated by special charter of the Legislature in 1818. It embraces in its membership employers and employes. Its objects are clearly defined in its constitution to be "the relief of sick and superannuated members; the cultivation of feelings of mutual friendship and respect between employers and journeymen; and general intellectual improvement." The Society presents no untried, youthful record. Nor is it egotism to claim that in the more than sixty years of its existence, it has made a meritorious history and been a power for good. It has exerted a beneficial influence upon our art. It has done much to soften the asperities which too often exist between workmen and employers. Meeting in the rooms of the Society on a common level, it has united them in the bonds of mutual esteem—harmonizing differences and breaking down the antagonism which class-organization so frequently stimulates between capital and labor. For it is when men come together for mutual benefit that each best learns the moral worth of the other, and thus are more kindly disposed to consider the relative rights of all. The members have been faithful to the suffering and the aged in all these years, and carefully laid their remains in the tomb at death; they have comforted the widow and orphans in their desolation; they have provided intellectual food by social meetings and a library; and they have always kept a fund on hand to insure fidelity to their obligations.

That the Society has been a school for culture, and a stepping-stone to advancement, is proved by the eminent names on its roll of membership. If I uttered them, you would recognize many who have achieved a reputation creditable to themselves and honorable to our profession. They have gone out from us to fill places of distinction on the press, in science and literature, at the bar, on the bench, in the pulpit, the halls of legislation, and the marts of trade. So has their impress been felt in shaping the progress of society.

It is the great fact of our art that while it has all the elements of a purely mechanical pursuit, it also affords grand opportunity for the expression of the highest intellectual culture and genius. It is true that the large majority of printers never rise above the lower plane; it is equally true that no craft opens so many avenues to those who have the ambition to make for themselves a name and a place among the world's noblest and best benefactors.

In the midst of the gloom and slumber of the Dark Ages, which long had held the mass of men in vassalage to ignorance, superstition, and tyranny,

> "Earth heard the mandate from the skies,
> Let there be light — great Art, arise!"

The men who were identified with printing in its earlier history were from the learned of their times; yet the title of printer added lustre to their scholastic reputation. It was a passport to social position among the nobility. Wealth, distinctions, orders, were lavished upon them. Kings and nobles sought to do them honor, believing themselves ennobled by becoming "patrons of the art."

Kings, Lords, and Commons for centuries had constituted the "three estates" of governments, but as the Art of Printing diffused the light of knowledge, and books were multiplied, there arose a "fourth estate" in the Press. Every form of indignity, oppression, and tyranny that ingenuity could invent has been employed to arrest its power and crush out its existence. Yet steadily it has gained and irresistibly held an augmenting sway, until now, with the imperial dignity of the first estate, the Press dares to dictate the policy of governments, to invoke and guide revolutions, to overthrow dynasties; yea, through its omnipresent spirit, to mould the entire fabric of society.

Thus does the Press, concentrating the voice of the people, proclaim its decrees to be observed by kings and all in authority. The Press has, indeed, a mighty mission, as the exponent of all the agencies to advance and establish the welfare of man. May it always be consecrated to the maintenance of the right, keeping its liberty free from license and its balance of censorship always just, and, with its ever-expanding resources, spread far and wide the blessings of civilization and Christianity.

Professor Morse, we welcome your participation in this scene; for no hand was deemed so worthy to lift the veil as yours. Franklin caught the electric thought from Heaven; but it was reserved for you to yoke its untamed power to the service of industry and intelligence. Wherever the iron nerves traverse the earth, there will be known and linked the names of Franklin and Morse.

Albert De Groot, we thankfully receive this deed of trust from your hands; and we pledge ourselves and our successors to guard it with the vigilance of love. May God bless you for your noble gift!

This acceptance by Mr. Savage concluded the exercises, which, notwithstanding the sharp wintry wind, were listened to attentively. The Band then played Auld Lang Syne, and the multitude slowly dispersed; but a smaller assembly continued in admiring attendance, at the foot of the Statue, during the entire day.

VIII

The Banquet.

THE banquet in the evening, at Delmonico's, on Fourteenth street, was largely attended. The arrangements were excellent, and reflected great credit on the committee. Every guest, on entering the reception-parlor, was presented with a diagram of the banquet-hall, with his name opposite an appropriate seat at the table. All confusion was thus avoided. The guests began to assemble in the parlors as early as six o'clock, but the hour of seven had arrived before they were marshalled into the dining-room. Plates were laid for 136, and there were few vacant places. At a table on a raised dais, and running lengthwise, were seated those of the guests whom the committee most delighted to honor. To the reporters of the different daily papers excellent places were assigned, near the speakers. The room was tastefully decorated with bunting, and the tables were beautifully ornamented. Of the dinner itself, it is sufficient praise to say that it was in Delmonico's best style. The Rev. Dr. S. Irenæus Prime presided, supported on his right by Captain De Groot, and on his left by Horace Greeley. Among the many distinguished guests present were A. Oakey Hall, Rev. Henry Ward Beecher, Rev E. H. Chapin, Peter Cooper, Erastus Brooks, Rev. Robert Duane, Robert Hoe, J. H. Anthon, Benjamin Franklin Bache, and H. O. Houghton, of the Riverside Press, Cambridge. The six long tables were filled with printers and journalists, who were generally well known in the trade and to each other. This intimacy of acquaintance had the happiest result. Every one seemed anxious to contribute to the general entertainment. From the beginning there was a noticeable absence of the restraint and formality too common at public dinners.

The annexed diagram is a copy of the arrangement of seats, as made by the committee. The few exchanges desired were quickly effected, and without disorder.

THE ARRANGEMENT OF SEATS.

29 27 25 23 21 19 17 15 13 11 9 7 5 3 1 2 4 6 8 10 12 14 16 18 20 22 24 26 28

31 TABLE No. 1 30

6		4		2		3		5	
21	20	21	20	21	20	21	20	21	20
19	18	19	18	19	18	19	18	19	18
17	16	17	16	17	16	17	16	17	16
15	14	15	14	15	14	15	14	15	14
13	12	13	12	13	12	13	12	13	12
11	10	11	10	11	10	11	10	11	10
9	8	9	8	9	8	9	8	9	8
7	6	7	6	7	6	7	6	7	6
5	4	5	4	5	4	5	4	5	4
3	2	3	2	3	2	3	2	3	2
1		1		1		1		1	

TABLE No. 1.

1 Rev. Dr. Prime.	9 J. T. H. Ward.	17 F. J. Ottarson.	25 Rev. J. A. Spencer.
2 Horace Greeley.	10 Judge Spencer.	18 G. W. Matsell.	26 Peter C. Baker.
3 Capt. De Groot.	11 Erastus Brooks.	19 Sinclair Tousey.	27 H. C. Bowen.
4 Peter Cooper.	12 Robert Hoe.	20 Thos. N. Rooker.	28 C. A. Alvord.
5 A. Oakey Hall.	13 Robert Bonner.	21 Wm. Orton.	29 J. B. Ford.
6 Rev. E. H. Chapin.	14 J. M. Vanderlip.	22 Rev. Dr. Duane.	30 H. O. Houghton.
7 Rev. H. W. Beecher.	15 W. H. Hurlbert.	23 Dr. B. F. Bache.	31 John F. Trow.
8 J. H. Anthon.	16 O. Ottendorfer.	24 John Mullaly.	

TABLE No. 2.

1 DOUGLAS TAYLOR.	7 N. D. BANGS.	12 Mr. THOMAS.	17 GEORGE MATHER.
2 I. W. ENGLAND.	8 I. LANDIS.	13 S. E. MORSE, Jr.	18 TIMES REPORTER.
3 J. HOWARD, JR.	9 E. L. GAUL.	14 SAMUEL SINCLAIR.	19 TRIBUNE REPORTER
4 H. PALMER	10 F. MIERSON.	15 R. N. PERLEE.	20 SUN REPORTER.
5 AUG. DALY.	11 W. J. HILL.	16 ORANGE JUDD.	21 REPORTER.
6 S. G. COURTNEY.			

TABLE No. 3.

1 JAMES L. SMITH.	7 J. M. CONNER.	12 M. K. PELLETREAU.	17 BENJAMIN WOOD.
2 CHARLES GAYLER.	8 S. K. DEVIS.	13 A. LITTLE.	18 F. E. WILLIAMS.
3 S. CANTRELL.	9 F. STREET.	14 D. E. GAVITT.	19 W. H. BRAY.
4 A. D ATKINSON.	10 M. F. GALE.	15 J. G. LIGHTBODY.	20 HERALD REPORTER.
5 E. O. JENKINS.	11 D. D. T. MOORE.	16 J. C. HOWARD.	21 EXPRESS REPORTER.
6 W. C. CONNER.			

TABLE No. 4.

1 J. F. BALDWIN.	7 W. C. MARTIN.	12 M. BELL.	17 JAMES LINDSAY.
2 J. H. SMITH.	8 H. C. LANIUS.	13 Mr. ROBERTS.	18 J. H. VAN EVRIE.
3 T. L. DE VINNE.	9 A. CAMPBELL.	14 SHELDON COLLINS.	19 I. W. MACK.
4 HENRY SPEAR.	10 FRANK LESLIE.	15 GUEST.	20 WORLD REPORTER.
5 H. D. WADE.	11 T. H. SENIOR.	16 GUEST.	21 J. POLHEMUS.
6 A. VANDERBURGH.			

TABLE No. 5.

1 D. GODWIN.	7 D. H. JONES.	12 G. T. CROWELL.	17 P. S. HOE.
2 D. W. BRUCE.	8 A. D. FARMER.	13 S. M. ISAACS.	18 H. C. PAGE.
3 R. J. GODWIN.	9 C. F. FRAZIER.	14 L. FRANCIS.	19 Mr. RUSSELL.
4 REV. E. S. PORTER.	10 M. M. POMEROY.	15 Mr. COTTRELL.	20 W. HAGAR.
5 B. BRANDRETH.	11 C. C. SAVAGE.	16 GUEST.	21 GUEST.
6 S. GODWIN.			

TABLE No. 6.

1 GEORGE P. ROWELL.	7 T. P. ROBERTS.	12 P. FITZPATRICK.	17 GUEST.
2 CHARLES N. KENT.	8 PAUL LOESER.	13 FRANK QUEEN.	18 F. BANGS.
3 SAMUEL FRENCH.	9 DWIGHT ROBERTS.	14 GUEST.	19 WILLIAM EVERDELL.
4 JOHN A. MOORE.	10 GUSTAV HEIN.	15 GUEST.	20 C. R. STETSON.
5 Mr. GARDINER.	11 GUEST.	16 GUEST.	21 ALEXANDER STETSON.
6 HERMAN UHL.			

A blessing was invoked by the Rev. Dr. Porter. At the plate of each guest was placed a copy of the Pennsylvania Gazette, of September 10, 1741, "printed by B. Franklin, Postmaster, at the new printing-office near the market." This was an exact reprint of the original, and was presented by the American Photo-Lithographic Company. The bill of fare, comprising all the courses for which the distinguished caterer is so famous, was placed before each guest, and every one was eloquent in praise of the completeness of the dinner.

THE TOASTS AND SPEECHES.

At the conclusion of the dinner, the Chairman, Rev. Dr. S. Irenæus Prime, arose and asked attention to the reading of the Toasts, and to the responses which were to be made. In introducing the intellectual entertainment of the evening, Dr. Prime made a most effective and agreeable speech. The words are here given; but they convey no idea of the felicitous manner of the speaker, or of the irresistibly humorous vein in which he spoke. He seemed to put every guest in the best possible mood for enjoyment, and by his happy manner, in his opening words, largely contributed in making this part of the banquet one of the most notable ever held within Delmonico's walls.

Dr. Prime said:

It is one hundred and sixty-six years to-day since a boy was born (we have his own words for it) in Boston, New England, whose birth and memory we are met to celebrate to-night.

I have not the least idea of giving you a biographical sketch of that child and of that man, and yet it may be that it will be new to some of you that he was the youngest son of the youngest son for five successive generations, and that he was the fifteenth child out of seventeen. He began his illustrious career as a candle-maker. If he had stuck to it, no doubt he would have made a great light in the world—but then he would have had less to do with lightning. We follow him from the candle-maker's shop to the printing-office of his brother, and then we find him making street-ballads in Boston; and his most sensible father checked him in his mad career as a poet, by telling him that verse-makers were always miserable beggars—and so he was saved from that. Next we find him in Philadelphia eating, as he says himself, a puffy roll in the street, which he bought for a cent—bought three of them, by the way, for three cents, but having found one sufficient for his breakfast, he gave away the other two loaves to a woman and child who were poorer than he. He was seen eating these rolls by Miss Reed, who afterward became Mrs. Benjamin Franklin; and when he fell in love with Miss Reed he began to rise in the world. And so, gentlemen, if that Reed was ever shaken in the wind, it was still enough to sustain him in the future struggles of life.

Gentlemen, this young man—I speak now to many of the rising aspirants for distinction in the press—this young man, beginning his career of writing for the press, passed his communications under the sill of the door of his father's office. So modest was he, that he was unwilling even to have it known that he was the author of these productions. What modesty distinguished the writers of the press of that day! There is nothing like it among us. Now, when a young man sets out upon this career—I have been thirty years on the press, and have seen many of them—he goes in boldly and opens the door, and says, "What will you give me for that?" Not so with our illustrious father and friend, the great prototype of the Franklins of the present day.

Now, I have no idea of following him throughout that career, which afterward became so illustrious. Far be it from me to undertake to say all the bright and remarkable things that are to be said to-night. But, gentlemen, there is only one name in the history of our country that we would name before that of Benjamin Franklin, and that is the name over all American names, the name of George Washington. And I regard it as a most astonishing fact, that the city of New York, distinguished as it is in its literature, in the enjoyment of a press—if I didn't belong to it myself, I would say—a press unrivalled by that of any other city in the world—it is to me a most astonishing fact, that we have lived to this day without seeing in our city a Statue of Benjamin Franklin, and that we are now permitted to be indebted for that Statue, not to the munificence and gratitude of the press itself, but to our illustrious guest this evening, Captain De Groot. It is, therefore, an occasion of the highest enjoyment which has called us together to-night, and I ask you without further words of introduction to receive the sentiments which have been prepared, which I will, from time to time, offer to you, and call upon various gentlemen present to respond, whom I know you will be delighted to listen to. I regret to say that the President of the United States was not able to come to-night—to be with us. He regrets it amazingly, and will the more when he knows what a good time we had.

I propose the first sentiment, and that we rise and drink standing to the toast—

THE PRESIDENT OF THE UNITED STATES.

The toast was drank standing. After the Band had played a national air, the Chairman again rose and said:

Gentlemen, I have now the pleasure to give you—

THE STATE OF NEW YORK AND THE CITY OF NEW YORK.

And I will call upon his Honor the Mayor to respond to this sentiment.

His Honor A. Oakey Hall responded to this sentiment. On rising, he was received with long continued applause. He said:

Gentlemen:

I thank you most gratefully for this reception, and I accept it as a proof that you are not willing to discharge an old compositor because he has mixed his type a little in his form, nor to wholly ignore an old compositor because he has slept while the devil ran away with his copy. To-day the city which you have toasted beheld Franklin's Statue unveiled. Last summer she witnessed the dedication of another to Morse. The first one faces the newspaper temples, wherein public opinion finds shrines; the other confronts newspaper readers, who daily throng Central Park, from the skating newsboy to the sauntering student.

But why these statues in the antithetical contemplation? Is it not that the distance between the down-town statue and the up-town one—at topographical points that also mark the material growth of the city from the era at which Franklin died to the epoch in which Morse still honorably survives—that this distance may represent the intervening and crowded space in history between the first and eldest ally of newspaper enterprise, or between the hand printing-press and the electric telegraph—between the lightning experiments of Franklin and the electric utilizations of Morse? The presence of these two statues in this crowded metropolis will ever emphasize an old text, and indeed paraphrase it. "He who runneth may read" thrilling references to the march of human intelligence.

The spectacle this day witnessed in Printing-House Square will become historical in the annals of the State and city—Morse unveiling the Statue of Franklin! It was as if Herschel had dedicated a monument to Copernicus; or Hoe one to Caxton; or Faraday or John W. Draper another to Roger Bacon; or Cyrus McCormick one to Locatella; or Elias Howe, Jr. to Elias Growse, the German of the sixteenth century; or Beecher to St. Paul.

But let not the city forget the individual to whose æsthetic industry she owes the Statue of to-day; who has before aided in adorning a metropolis too much devoted to mere money-getting. There was once a German alchemist named Albert Groot, surnamed Albertus Magnus. It is said that he amalgamated the first bronze. He has a worthy namesake of to-day, and I close by giving you "The Health of Albert De Groot—a very Prince Magnus Albert among the royal good fellows of New York enterprise.

After Mayor Hall had concluded, the Chairman again commanded attention, and said:

Gentlemen, as we stood around this Statue that has been unveiled to-day, we saw sitting at its base one who bears a striking resemblance in some respects to the Statue itself. I think he must have been dull who did not see, and he must have been very phlegmatic who did not feel it. I was impressed, as I stood and beheld the resemblance. Therefore, I give you the third sentiment:

BENJAMIN FRANKLIN. *Printer, philosopher, diplomatist, and statesman. Perfected in the art of Printing, he soon became perfect in that knowledge which blended the greatest wisdom in national things with the highest statesmanship and truest philanthropy.*

I know that you will say at once that there is no other here whom I should call upon to respond to this sentiment than the "later Franklin," our old friend, Horace Greeley.

After the exciting and long-continued applause which followed had subsided, Mr. Greeley replied:

Mr. Chairman and Gentlemen:

If I were required to say for which of Franklin's achievements he deserved most and best of mankind, I should award the palm to his autobiography—so frank, so sunny, so irradiated by a brave, blithe, hearty humanity. For if our fathers had not—largely by the aid of his counsel, his labors, his sacrifices—achieved their independence at the first effort, they would have tried it again and again until they did achieve it; if he had not made his immortal discovery of the identity of electricity with the lightning, that truth would nevertheless have at length been demonstrated. But if he had not so modestly and sweetly told us how to wrestle with poverty and compel opportunity, I do not know who beside would or could have done it so well. There is not to-day, there will not be in this nor in the next century, a friendless, humble orphan, working hard for naked daily bread, and glad to improve his leisure hours in the corner of a garret, whom that biography will not cheer and strengthen to fight the battle of life buoyantly and manfully. I wish some humane tract society would present a copy of it to every poor lad in the United States.

But I must not detain you. Let me sum up the character of Franklin in the fewest words that will serve me. I love and revere him as a journeyman printer who was frugal and didn't drink; a *parvenu* who rose from want to competence, from obscurity to fame, without losing his head; a statesman who did not crucify mankind with long-winded documents or speeches; a diplomatist who did not intrigue; a philosopher who never bored; and an office-holder who didn't steal. So regarding him, I respond to your sentiment with "Honor to the memory of Franklin."

At the close of Mr. Greeley's response, the Chairman again rose and said:

Gentlemen, I know that you will be glad when I tell you upon whom I am about to call for a response to this sentiment:

HONESTY THE BEST POLICY. *One of Franklin's earliest and best maxims; illustrated in his life and supporting him in death: a maxim worthy of all time, all nations, and all professions.*

And *facile princeps* in the profession to which I belong, I beg to name and to ask our friend and guest, the Rev. Henry Ward Beecher, to respond.

Mr. Beecher was received with great applause. When silence was at length restored, Mr. Beecher said:

I am a little at a loss to know which profession you refer to. I am a clergyman sometimes—and I am an editor also. I have been connected with newspapers, I may say, all my life. However, I accept the courtesy which you show me, whether it is in one profession or in the other; for lately they have become so conjoined that it is difficult to tell whether a man is preaching or printing. A great deal of printing goes to preaching and a great deal of preaching goes out in printing, and to that I attribute the reformation which has taken place in the world, and notably in this city. We are all of us so much of one mind on this subject that my discourse will have all the merit of an orthodox sermon. Everybody believes it before the minister begins, everybody knows what he is going to say, and everybody goes to sleep before he gets through.

I have heard it frequently said that this maxim of Franklin's was not the correct one, and not equal to that of the Greeks, who held that no motive should be addressed to man except that which reaches their higher faculties. It is said that honesty never should have been propounded as the best policy: that it was teaching men to act so from the meanest of considerations. I have no objection whatever that men should be honest and truthful from a consideration of the eternal fitness of things; but as there is only one in ten thousand that understands this eternal fitness of things, what are we to do? Not excluding these men of higher refinement, I for one am heartily thankful that Franklin gave currency to this maxim, which, instead of reducing toil to a lower level, has a tendency to elevate it; for, however high you may soar, honesty is the place where you must start. The men that attain permanent success must also, in the nature of things, be honest; that is, they must observe faith between man and man, without which there cannot be friendship or honor, and the affairs of life cannot run without running off the track. I believe that we can give to our common people this maxim, and when it has made the universal ground of action it has laid the foundation of that stability of character which has made our people what they are—not simply industrious or frugal, but made them a true speaking people and a fair dealing people. I do not doubt that there are a great many persons who slip up, and mistake, to call it by no stronger term than that; and I do know that there are a great many persons who at one period of life or another believe that they know the trick at wrestling by which they can throw fortune; but I do not believe that any man that has been on the stage of life for forty years will say, whether he did tell bouncers or not at some period of it, that those were the things which won, and will also say that the things which did win were clear thinking, honest dealing, and true speaking. That man that comes through in the end, and achieves fortune and enjoys his gain, that man at the bottom has been an honest man. So much for my first profession.

Now, as to my second, I feel that any further remark is entirely superfluous; for if there be one calling that entirely reverences truth, it is that of the newspaper men. If there be one thing that we are more proud of than another, it is fair dealing between man and man. We are particular as to our facts; we sort them, we present them so that they shall strike the imagination right, and we are especially careful of our words, that they may measure the truth carefully—no more, no less. Though there are uncharitable people who do say things hard to be borne, yet I may say that all newspapers which affect to prosper, and whose proprietors, instead of shinning the street for funds, are laying up money for themselves, have been those that in the main were fair-dealing, truth-telling newspapers. In regard to those that do not speak the truth, I have only this to say, with your hearty concurrence: May they never be able to save money; and may the time speedily come when the followers of Franklin shall be as prompt as he was, as fair as he was, love truth as much as he did—and then if there be but few newspapers remaining, those that do remain will be all the better for it.

After Mr. Beecher had concluded, the Chairman said:

Gentlemen, I have the greatest pleasure in now proposing to you the fifth toast:

OUR FRIEND AND OUR GUEST, CAPTAIN ALBERT DE GROOT. *He has done for the memory of Franklin and the printers of New York what we and they should long ago have done in honor of our own craft and profession.*

Gentlemen, will you rise, and give three cheers for Captain De Groot?

The cheers were given with a will, and then Captain De Groot replied:

My Friends:

Certainly you will not expect a speech from me. I never have been guilty of it; that belongs to others more capable than myself. But, perhaps, on this occasion it may not be out of place for me to say a few words.

It is now some two years since Mr. Baker, as we were standing in Printing-House Square, pointed yonder where the Statue of Franklin now stands, and expressed the wish that he might see a statue erected there to the memory of Franklin. The suggestion met my views; it flourished in my mind; and I saw that I might have an opportunity of doing that which I had long wished to do—make a return to the press for many favors received at its hands: for I had known many of its members during the greater part of my life, and they had been kind and indulgent to me during my public life on the Hudson River. And so I thought the matter over for a while, and I consulted with some of the leading members of the press—with Mr. Bennett, Mr. Brooks, Mr. Dana, and several others—and laid my views before them. They seemed to be pleased with the idea and gave me encouragement, and said that there was no doubt but that the printers would accept it with great pleasure. I resolved at once upon the work. I secured the services of Mr. Plassman, an eminent sculptor, and the result you have had before you to-day.

I sincerely wish that some one more worthy than myself may build monuments and build works of art to all good men who have done so much for our country. I now propose "The Memory of Franklin."

Drank standing, and in silence. The Chairman then rose, and remarked:

Gentlemen, we have the honor of two guests to-night who are direct descendants of the illustrious Franklin, and I shall request Rev. Dr. Duane, of Brooklyn, to give us the pleasure of looking on his face and hearing his voice.

The Rev. Dr. Duane, as a lineal descendant of Franklin, was received with real enthusiasm. He said:

There is an elder representative of the family present, who modestly desires me to respond. I suppose it is because he has been a doctor, and, to use an old joke, while I preached he practiced. I can only say that those who are the great-grandchildren of Franklin endeavor to appreciate the privilege which is theirs. My mother, who lived to the age of eighty-one, remembered most distinctly her illustrious grandfather, and often spoke of him, particularly how she used to be allowed to go into his study to read or play if she did not disturb him.

Dr. Duane also exhibited two miniature portraits preserved in the family, one of Franklin, taken by order of Louis XIV.; the other of the grand monarch, and presented by the king to the American patriot. This last was the picture referred to in Franklin's Will, set with four hundred and eight diamonds. Dr. Duane gave an interesting account of this picture, and explained that although the diamonds had been removed, yet they had never passed out of the possession of the family.

The Chairman again requested attention, and said:

Gentlemen, I shall now propose to you the sixth toast—the loyal sentiment—

> OUR COUNTRY. *Immense in its area and wonderful in its growth. It needs but true men in service and in council to outlive all the republics of history.*

And I am sure that every eye will turn for a fitting response to our *universal* favorite and friend, Rev. Dr. Chapin.

The Doctor rose amid the most tremendous cheers, and said:

I cannot say that the theme held out to me is a narrow one, or that I would probably stray from the subject; for I could hardly get outside of it. The embarrassment arises from the difficulty of compressing what might be said into the limits of an after-dinner speech.

After all, let us do justice to the feeling which prompts the sentiment just announced, and let no man be ashamed of the enthusiasm that leaps into his heart and leaps from his lips at the utterance of those two simple words, "Our Country!" When he is ashamed, let his country, humanity, his own better nature, be ashamed of him. There was just as little to explain and just as little to apologize for in the love of country as there was for any other lawful affection. God planted it, as He has planted the instinct of childhood, love of home, and attachment to domestic life, among the inmost fibres of the human heart. It grows as the grass grows, as the flowers spring up spontaneously out of the soil everywhere, among the Alpine glaciers or the tropical palms. All the explanation we need give, or ought to expect to be given, of the sentiment is expressed in the familiar lines:

> "We love our land because it is our own,
> And scorn to give aught other reason why."

But over and above this natural love of country there is a matured estimation, a deliberate honoring of one's country, which rests on solid grounds of reason. This honoring of country has an historical significance, and is productive of that best of all crops that grows out of the native soil—good and great men. The final question concerning love of country must be, what has it contributed to human progress and human welfare? This is more than the natural beauty of a country or material wealth. Lives of useful achievement are more beautiful than fertile valleys, and memories of martyrs and heroes more precious than silver or gold. What has been the case in regard to our own country in this kind of productiveness? Have we been productive of the good and great? The other kind have grown rankly, and some have been blown down by the autumn gales, but no nation has produced such a remarkable cluster of men as those which gathered around the early period of the country, among its colonizers and founders; and among these is certainly the man to whom we do honor to-day. As was said to-night, there is but one name which is honored still higher. Perhaps there is no man who so truly represents America itself, its institutions, its ideas, its achievements, as Benjamin Franklin, or a more highly typical American. Channing was delighted to hear beyond the Alps his country called the land of Franklin. He is a type of its solid, its material achievement, the foundation of all others. We do not ascribe to Franklin the highest elements. In short, we have acted in the practical and solid spirit of Franklin himself. So with the common sense of the nation, its clear discernment of end to means. All this is very much in Franklin's character, and he stands as a type of it—a type of the versatility of our people—and in nothing more than in the department of scientific investigation.

It was eminently proper, as has been stated, that this should be expressed in the significant relation of Morse unveiling the Statue. It was fit that the man of the wire should unveil the face of the man of the key and kite-string; fit that the man who made the lightning tick should show us the image of the man who made the lightning come, and whose magnificent induction was after all the first step toward the invention which is destined to transmute this globe into one common brain and one universal heart.

Franklin was a representative type of this country also in the characteristic that an opportunity is given every man to rise and better himself if he can. Agassiz said he asked himself the question, what was the difference between the institutions of the Old World and this? And he found it to be, that in Europe everything was done to maintain the rights of the few, while in America everything was done to make a man of anybody who has the elements of humanity in him. Franklin was the type of the opportunity given in this country for a man to rise alone to the highest attainment. But let nobody suppose he can be Benjamin Franklin. The speeches made to schoolboys, averring that if they persevered any one of them might become President of the United States, should be thoroughly detested. They can be in a great deal better business sometimes than be President of the United States. But one thing Benjamin Franklin did every man can do. Every step he took, he took faithfully; and every piece of work he did, he did well. He went onward and upward, until the candle the poor boy lit in the chandler's shop illuminated the world, and he became the most eminent in council and the most royal in the presence of kings. Franklin, too, illustrates the principle of patriotism which is at the core of the American heart when called for. This country has always had men ready for the emergency, who now stand in long lines in the records of national remembrance and achievement.

Franklin was not a very poetical or romantic man. I do not think we are a very romantic or poetical people. But let each nation do its specific work. Let the European nations fulfill their destiny; let it be ours to organize liberty, to clear away old rubbish, to gather together the elements of human welfare and progress with the large wisdom and practical skill of Benjamin Franklin, and put them in working order. Be it ours to unroll the grand idea of the people so fitly illustrated by him who passed through every rank of public experience; be it ours, with practical genius, to scatter wide free institutions.

The next sentiment in order was—

PUBLIC OPINION. *To be respected when it is stable, consistent, and upon the side of law and order, and to be discarded when governed by caprice or passion, malice or revenge.*

This toast was not responded to, but in lieu thereof Mr. Hill sang "Our Country," and Mr. Levy performed two airs on the cornet; at the conclusion of which, the Chairman rose and said:

Gentlemen, I will now give you the next toast—

THE PRESS. *While its conductors owe to each other the courtesy and charity of true gentlemen, they owe to the public the diffusion of knowledge founded upon truth, and with their best intelligence unscrupulous rectitude. "It is not enough that men mean well: it becomes them to do well."*

And I shall request a gentleman to respond who, in his journal and in his life, illustrates the dignity, the integrity, and the fidelity that should distinguish the press—the Hon. Erastus Brooks.

Mr. Brooks rose amid great cheering, and said:

Mr. President, and Gentlemen:

At this hour of the evening, after the eloquent addresses of the day and of the night, I feel that I have neither wit, worth, nor words suitably to respond to the toast which has been received with so much favor. If I follow your example, sir, as a journalist, I must be silent: for you have said that modesty forbade you, as one of the profession, to speak for the press; and if I take the hint given in the speech of the reverend gentleman beside me [Rev. Mr. Beecher], the press has been spoken of and to already. When Thomas Jefferson first went to the Court of Versailles, and presented his credentials as the successor of Franklin, "You replace Dr. Franklin," was the greeting of the Count de Vergennes to Jefferson. "I succeed Franklin," said Jefferson; "no one can replace him." It is my fortune, or rather my misfortune, to-night to follow the distinguished orators who have gone before me. But, sir, as it is a part of the programme of the occasion that I should speak for the Press, its courtesies, powers, and duties, I must do so, as best I may, with a brevity becoming the hour of the night.

All honor, then, to the day! All honor to the memory of Franklin, and all honor to the generous donor who has reared a monument worthy of the occasion. We are living just now almost in an epoch of monuments. The several States are rearing them in the form of statues of their own illustrious statesmen and heroes, to be placed in the new Museum of Art, the old Hall so many years used by the Representatives of the people in the city of Washington. We have a monument now to Franklin placed on Printing-House Square, with another to Morse on Central Park, and still others there and on other parks of the city. Boston, where Franklin was born, has her Franklin monument, and the city of Philadelphia, for half a century his home, has hers also; but without disparagement to either, the monument unveiled to-day far eclipses them in grandeur and completeness. We see the man as he was in the fullness of years and in the meridian of his power. We recall the life of one who said in mature years what very few men have ever said or thought, that he would be quite willing to live his life over again, asking only the privilege common to all authors and editors, of improving the second edition.

Journalism, Mr. President, in those days had no second, third, fourth, and more editions, so common to the newspapers of the present day. No; the old journals were printed upon a half-sheet of foolscap, as was the Boston News-Letter in 1704, and the Boston Gazette & Courant of 1719. Then indeed, even weekly newspapers were among the wonders of the country, and the news from Europe was published at home five and six months after date. But Franklin owed fame and fortune to the press. He learned to write for it as Charles Dickens and so many others after him learned to write and to print. What he composed, as has been said, was not only stealthily conveyed, in his youth, to the office of the diminutive journal which his brother printed, but his compositions were the result of deep thought and hard labor. He read thoughtfully chapters of the Spectator and De Foe, and then wrote out what he remembered from Addison's letters, in order to improve his memory and his style. So, also, he cultivated his imagination by reading John Bunyan. His father's maxim was taken from that memorable text of King Solomon: "Seest thou a man diligent in his calling; He shall stand before kings; He shall not stand before mean men." And this parental precept Franklin obeyed to the letter. No man was more diligent in the pursuit of knowledge, and no man ever better illustrated the maxim that "Knowledge is power." And Franklin not only lived to stand before kings, but in his own right and as a representative man, he was every inch a sovereign.

Franklin also was pre-eminently a practical man and a great discoverer. The mayor and people of a great city like this can understand what it was over a century since to establish a city Fire Department; to light and pave a city; to build up a circulating and subscription library; to found a hospital for the sick; a university of learning; a philosophical society for men of science; a forum for debating questions of State, of political economy, and of social life—and Franklin did all this in the city of his home, and before any other person there or elsewhere in the country. And whatever Franklin did was well done. His grandfather would have made him a student of theology at the age of eight or nine years; and if he had studied theology he would have been, as far as human wisdom goes, perfect in his calling. His maxim was to do all things well, alike in the printing-house, the shop, the Assembly; in the colony, abroad, at home, for the government at large, and by fair means every way and everywhere to win success.

And hence, Mr. President, his great success as a journalist. He was eminently courteous and forbearing, and remembered the wisdom and power of Him who said, "Though I speak with the tongues of men and of angels and have not charity, I am become as a sounding brass and a tinkling cymbal." And pardon me here for saying, in the presence of the whole newspaper press, and as one among the oldest of the profession present, that in my judgment the Press always loses its power and usefulness and becomes degraded when it ceases to be courteous. The tongue of scandal and the pen of calumny spring from the same source. Every display of passion and temper, of bitterness and anger, are unworthy of our calling and no part of our duty. The journal, years gone by, was wisely called "the history of the world for one day," and as such it ought to be a truthful history of that day and the times. Its true vocation is far beyond a mere record of intelligence, important as this is. Its purpose is—

"To show Virtue her own feature,
Scorn her own image—
And the very age and body of the time
Its form and pressure."

Franklin was called a free-thinker, and in one sense he was; but it was Franklin who said that nothing was so likely to win good fortune as personal virtue. He read Shaftsbury and Collins, it is true; but he was not a free-thinker in the sense of either of these authors. Like ourselves, he did not believe in an established State religion, and was tolerant with all religious creeds. He was tolerant, also, of all political thought and action, always excepting the creed of priestcraft over men and kingcraft over a free people. His free-thinking made him remember that he only was "a freeman whom the truth made free," and like him I would be as sorry to see a Press combined with all on one side in politics or creeds as I would be sorry to behold men all of one form of faith or one baptism in religion; for wherever on earth there is supreme power, be it in Church or State, there is despotism and an abuse of power. Franklin loved liberty in council, freedom in action, and national justice and independence. Before kings, lords, and commons, and prime ministers, he denounced all stamp acts and taxes which were not founded upon full equality, fair representation, and personal justice. Such men, Mr. President, never die. The pulse may cease to beat, the eyes close in death, the human form divine be imprisoned in its coffin, and, followed by weeping friends, borne to

> "The deep, damp vault,
> The mattock and the grave."

But men, wise, tolerant, philanthropic, and patriotic, like Franklin, never die. As we have seen to-day—

> "'Tis the sunset of life gives them mystical lore.
> And coming events cast their shadows before."

And now, to close, permit me to give you as a sentiment, "Toleration in the Press, in the pulpit, in public life and social life," always remembering, with Jefferson, that "error of opinion ceases to be dangerous when reason is left to combat it."

At the conclusion of Mr. Brooks' speech, the Chairman again requested attention, and said:

Gentlemen, I now propose, as the next sentiment—

THE WORKING PRESS. *From the old Ramage press used by Franklin, with two pulls to one form, to the eight and ten cylinder of our own Robert Hoe and the self-feeding press of Bullock. The first came from old England, and by hard hand-labor worked off one or two hundred impressions an hour. We send the last to Europe, with a capacity of printing twenty thousand and twenty-five thousand copies an hour.*

And when we toast the Working Press, you will all look to the one to whom, next to Captain De Groot, we are indebted for the Franklin Statue. He has *worked* at it, and *pressed* it forward, as a member of the working press, and now we would like to hear how it was done. I shall therefore introduce to you Mr. Peter C. Baker.

Mr. Baker was hailed with loud and repeated cheers. He said that as special reference had been made to his connection with the Statue, he preferred to speak of that, and begged to suggest that his friend, Mr. C. A. Alvord—a lover and a doer of "good work"—should be invited to respond to the "Working Press." This suggestion was received with favor, and Mr. Baker proceeded to speak as follows.

Mr. Chairman and Gentlemen:

Perhaps I may be permitted here to express the great gratification which I feel, now that the Statue is fixed in its place, there to stand immovably, I trust, for generations to come. When Captain De Groot agreed to give our profession a Statue of Franklin, I thought it was entirely safe for me to promise that the press and printers of this city would willingly provide a pedestal on which the figure should stand; and I am made happy this evening, and I know you will share my feelings of satisfaction when I tell you that the entire amount needed to defray every expense connected with our part of the programme is secured. Our noble Statue was unveiled this day free from any burden of debt over or under it. I have worked earnestly to be able to make this report to you this evening; and the generous manner in which I have generally been met by the newspaper press, and by those most closely connected with the printing business, has been to me truly a supreme pleasure. I really wish that the few who did not respond to my call could share the satisfaction which all who have contributed will feel whenever they pass the monument which now stands out so nobly in Printing-House Square.

I have no fear as to the verdict the public will pass upon this Statue. There have been too many gentlemen of the most cultivated tastes who have watched this work all through its progress, and finally pronounced it "very good," and worthy of Franklin, and worthy of our city, to make me uneasy as to what the people's opinion will be. True, there may be some who "are nothing if not critical," who may think they see too many or too few wrinkles in the coat, or who may suggest that this or that might have been better; but, take it all in all, I believe the general verdict will be that we have "Old Ben" in a very satisfactory shape, with a grand, good face, which clearly marks the great characteristics of his history—wisdom, benevolence, honesty, and sincerity. And we have him, too, in a garb which carries us back to the early history of our country—to the good old American gentleman, one of the olden time. And we have him, too, with his newspaper in his hand, representing the journal with which he was so long connected, and which was always noted for its courtesy, candor, and consistency. Besides, no one can mistake that the figure is Franklin's. Children, even, will instantly recognize it, and all the great virtues of the man will speak out from the bronze, and be a perpetual lesson for good to all who learn the history of the man thus honored in our time.

But even if our Statue shall not rank among the greatest works of art—as one in which the sculptor's genius, rather than his subject, commands our admiration—we must remember that our generous friend, De Groot, had no Phidias or Angelo to summon to his side. No such inspiration is given to modern artists. The great sculptors of the past, you remember, gained their immortal fame by giving the world their conceptions of gods rather than of men. But it would hardly answer the purpose of modern art to make Franklin other than he was—a man in form and figure much like many of us, with even his great grandchildren in our very midst this very evening.

Captain De Groot labored conscientiously, I know, to give us a Franklin which should be recognized and acknowledged as the true old philosopher, statesman, and printer, whose form and features every American carries in his mind. And Ernst Plassman, the sculptor, spared no labor to gather around him all the most reliable copies of form, face, and dress, which could be procured. Poor Plassman is weak and borne down by sickness to-night, and cannot be with us. He is an honest artist, and did his best to give us Franklin as we most love to see him. And so, too, with the same enthusiastic spirit, worked those who cast the figure in bronze, and the skilled workmen who chiseled and filed the face and figure after the metal came from the sculptor's model or mold. All, I believe, worked conscientiously, and with a love for the figure they were fashioning. And I hope the world will think they did well.

And now, another thought, and I close. It is not only as a printer that I am rejoiced we have this day unveiled a Statue of Franklin. It is almost as much as an American, and as a native of New York, that I feel a pride in this gift of Albert De Groot. I am encouraged to believe that other public-spirited citizens may do as our guest has done; and that ere long other public squares and parks of our city may be graced by statues of the great men who founded and who sought to perpetuate our free institutions. That the sturdy old merchant, John Hancock, whose bold signature alone is worth more than a volume of essays on courage and integrity; that Jefferson, whose immortal "truths" can never die; that our own Morris and Clinton; and the nation's great soldier, Scott; and gallant, glorious Harry Clay; and the majestic Webster, and others who have won their country's love, may stand, in marble or in bronze, before us, and before the generations yet to come, illustrating the value of a noble, unselfish life; and deepening still deeper that spirit of patriotism and love of human virtue which keeps a people pure, and are the strongest supports to sustain free institutions.

Again I say, I thank De Groot for his generous gift, and for the great good influence it may exert in giving our city other statues of our country's benefactors.

At the conclusion of Mr. Baker's remarks, Mr. C. A. Alvord was called upon, and made an extremely interesting address, giving a history of the progress of printing from the hand-press on which Franklin worked to the ten-cylinder Hoe press. He said:

The Ramage Press was the first we had of any kind, and it was what we should call a small, ugly, insignificant affair, with screw power, and two pulls to a demy sheet; and yet this was the best press of the day, imported from England, and on it Franklin did all his printing. Next came the Stanhope, with one pull, and a platen of sufficient size to cover a medium form. Then the Columbian, or Clymer. These were all designed and made in England. Then came, of our own invention and manufacture, the Wells, the Smith, and many others; and at last the Rust, or Washington, which proved to be truly, like him whose name it bears, the chief; for even now, in this much advanced age, when old things have passed away and all things have become new, the Washington Hand Press, with the snug little hand-roller, the strong arm and the watchful eye, must be brought into constant requisition for the most skillful artistic work. A few of us have seen all of those antique concerns and still live. I have myself worked upon them all, back to the skin-ball and the coarse dip paper, and down to the composition hand-roller, the highly calendered paper, and the fine wood-cut, delicate and sharp as steel.

In the year 1790, William Nicholson took out a patent in England for a machine calculated to print rapidly, to meet in some measure the increasing demand for news; and, strange to say, his plan embraced the last successful idea of speed—that of placing the type upon the surface of a revolving cylinder, the inking to be given by another cylinder, and the impression by a third; but, though he had one good idea, he proved unequal to the task of perfecting the necessary combinations, and his press was never built.

In 1814, Konig, a German, built for Mr. Walter, of the London Times, two machines, which first successfully printed a newspaper at the unprecedentedly rapid rate of 1,100 impressions in an hour. This machine embodied most of the ideas of Nicholson; but the best one, that of placing the type upon a revolving cylinder, was abandoned for a bed surface, and a large cylinder for the impression.

In 1827, Applegath and Cowper built for the Times a press which printed from 4,000 to 5,000 in an hour; but the demand for newspapers had increased so much everywhere, that this rate of speed was entirely unsatisfactory, and only an aggravation. But the world was obliged to endure it until 1853, when Applegath constructed for this same tremendous "Thunderer" something prodigious, promising to immortalize all the Applegaths, St. George and the Dragon, and the great John Bull. This abortion was ingenious, complicated, and absurd; large as an ordinary dwelling-house, all its inking and impression machinery revolving vertically, while it received and discharged its paper horizontally. Yet this machine carried its type upon a large revolving cylinder with a series of revolving cylinders running upon its surface, each constituting a distinct press, dependent upon the central drum for its form and its impression, and printed 16,000 sheets in an hour.

While these improvements and inventions were ostentatiously and noisily going on in England, our more modest but equally ingenious and industrious friends here were studying, experimenting, making patterns, castings, presses, in fact, on the grand plan of the solar system, at great expense of time and dollars; but none of their experiments reached their nice ideas of perfection, until, one bright, sunny morning, Colonel Richard M. Hoe rose after a night of pleasant dreams (for he is a happy fellow), and, as the two met at the Sheriff Street Factory, Richard M. says, "Bob, we are on the wrong track; we must throw away all of these traps, and begin anew." "What," says the cool-headed financier, "after expending $50,000 experimenting; please tell me where the money is coming from to begin anew?" "Yes," says the Colonel; "if it were $100,000 thus spent, it would prove a good investment, and is worth much more than what it cost, for it has taught us what we don't want, and now I know I have got here (tapping his forehead with his finger) just what we *do* want, and the short cut to success, and the means of paying for it. I see our fortune nearer at hand than ever before." From that hour they progressed rapidly, and in six months William Swain had the first Lightning Press in his office printing the Philadelphia Ledger; and in a most astonishingly brief space, all the newspapers of large circulation in all our principal cities were printed upon the Lightning Press, at the rate of from 16,000 to 25,000 sheets an hour.

All this occurred in 1854 and 1855, and in 1856 Lloyd's London Weekly threw the Times into the shade by coming out with one of Hoe's Lightning Presses. In 1857, Mr. Walter became convinced that he must have the American invention, notwithstanding his prejudices, or confess himself behind his neighbors; so he proposed to Messrs. Hoe & Co., that they arrange with some English founder, as they call machinists there, to build and sell their machines in the English market, at the same time naming the celebrated Whitworth, of Manchester, the inventor of the Whitworth gun, and some other famous things. The arrangement was made, and in about three years Whitworth completed and set up two of the Americo-English presses in Mr. Walter's office; but notwithstanding Whitworth's reputation, his presses were poorly built, so that they broke frequently, to the great grief of Walter and the disgust of the inventor, for Hoe & Co. have now between forty and fifty of those presses running in Great Britain, built in New York, every one of which gives perfect satisfaction, while those at the Times office, and all others made by Whitworth, have been defective and unsatisfactory; yet they were superior to any other in Europe for speed and execution.

The Bullock Press, running in the Sun office, is also a very novel and perfect machine, printing very rapidly; without feeders running a roll of paper, and cutting the sheets as they leave the form.

Hoe & Co. have built and placed in the office of the Daily News, in this city, a machine still more startling than any heretofore mentioned, upon which it is claimed that 64,000 copies of that notable sheet are struck off in an hour.

And now, Mr. Chairman, hoping that you will consider it sufficient for the Working Press, that it has increased in speed from 200 to 64,000 copies in an hour in the last forty years, I leave it in your hands for further improvements.

I am fully aware that these statistics must be very dry at any time, and more especially so after the flowing of such brilliant minds as have been tapped in our presence this evening, but a touch of dullness is sometimes wholesome to make brilliancy more apparent. My peroration is briefly this: Benjamin Franklin discovered that electricity is the material from which lightning is made, and that it can be controlled and applied to useful purposes. S. F. Benjamin Morse has applied it to useful purposes, but has still left most of its power untouched and unknown. Now we need but one more Benjamin to close the scientific circle, by collecting quantities of the element for propelling all the machinery of future ages. It is quite ripe for our use if we are ready to receive it, with the great revolving earth for its balance-wheel, and the Maker of all things for chief engineer.

When Mr. Alvord had concluded, the Chairman rose and proposed, as the next sentiment:

OUR JUDGES. *May they judge righteous judgment, without fear and without favor, remembering that the Supreme Being is the Supreme Judge, and that all justice is founded upon truth and honor, equity and right.*

As no response was made to this toast, the Chairman called upon Mr. Henry Spear to sing the well-known festival song of Thackeray, "Dr. Luther," which he gave with fine effect, and which was received with continued applause.

The next toast was

AMERICAN LITERATURE.

With the vigor of Manhood,
And the freshness of Youth,
'Tis the offspring of Freedom—
The Champion of Truth.

This was responded to by Rev. Dr. E. S. Porter. He said:

Mr. Chairman and Gentlemen:

The hour is late. Each part of the banquet has been rich enough to satisfy alike the appetites of body and of mind; yet the sentiment which you have assigned me cannot be passed in silence.

Some tribute at least is due from the members of the press to their illustrious co-workers, the authors of our rich, varied, and comprehensive literature. As Benjamin Franklin was himself both printer and writer, a thinker and a man of action, respect for his memory must constantly have in view the inseparable relations between those who are co-partners in the realms of letters.

Were time at our disposal, we might speak of some of the characteristics of our national literature. It must, however, suffice to recall the general principle, that the real life of a nation expresses itself in its literature more distinctively than in its external institutions, customs, and manners; for all these are themselves created, shaped, and modified by prevalent currents of thought flowing through manifold literary channels.

Great as has been the enterprise of this still youthful nation, it may be well doubted whether its material achievements have equalled its intellectual; for consider, that from the beginning it has been the aim of our people to educate, at all points and in every portion of society. The result is, that there is a greater market for literature here than in any other country. The productions of American authorship, fruitful as they are, do not content a national mind that aims at nothing short of cosmopolitan knowledge. Hence, American literature actually embodies in itself the best literature of all nations and of all ages. True, it has not come to its ripe harvest; but the sowers are many, the field large, and the soil rich. It may be claimed, that in two departments, at least, American authorship deserves undisputed pre-eminence. Bancroft, Motley, Prescott, Sparks, and others, have treated of public affairs under the guidance of a philosophy which recognizes popular rights as the end of all just government. Our great publicists, Wharton, Story, and their co-laborers, have carried international law to a height of excellence which entirely eclipses the purely speculative or purely expedient systems which preceded them. It is to be said in conclusion, that the American Press has in the main shown a generous consideration of the rights and claims of authors. Our thinkers and writers are not left, like Sidney Smith and Henry Brougham, to cultivate letters on a porridge of oatmeal. Not only are they well paid, as a rule, for their productions, but once a year the magnates of the press assemble the knights of the pen, and entertain them at a sumptuous banquet, the like of which Poor Richard never saw. Yet a sound body is essential to a sound mind; and with this original reflection, we may now soon withdraw, to press the world's great interest on, with lightning for our tongue, steam for our servant, the Hoe cylinder for our daily prophet, and the New York Typographical Society as the champion and defender of American literature.

The Chairman now proposed the twelfth toast.

OUR MOTHERS AND OUR WIVES; OUR DAUGHTERS AND OUR SISTERS. *We respect all their rights, and may God bless them in all their relations. "He that would thrive must ask his wife."*

To this the Hon. H. O. Houghton, of the Riverside Press, now Mayor of Cambridge, responded. He said:

Mr. Chairman and Gentlemen:

At this late hour I can only add my cheerful testimony to the motives which prompted the open-handed munificence of erecting at once a testimonial and a memorial—a memorial of the dead, whose example shall be for the imitation of the living for generations to come; a testimonial to the living of a friendship fostered by the very cares and toils of a profession so long honored and advanced by the illustrious dead.

The sentiment to which I am called upon to respond contains, so to speak, a whole "body of divinity" of the philosophy of Poor Richard. That Franklin himself appreciated the benefit of his maxim, is apparent from the fact that he married as early and as often as he could, and was not only a better man after his marriage than before, but his real prosperity began immediately thereafter.

Regarding Franklin as the patron saint of the printers, I was a little surprised, in viewing the Statue to-day for the first time, to find that it was made to turn its back upon Printing-House Square. But, on reflection, I think the position was well chosen. His back, to be sure, is to the printers; but his face, with his outstretched hand, is directed toward the occupants of that magnificent pile of buildings in the Park, where the scales of justice are sometimes held with an uneven hand, warning them, by the very benignity of his countenance, and the significant gesture, pointing not only to the Gazette which he holds in his left hand, but to the thunderers beyond, that if they deviate the least hair's-breadth from the rule of honesty, that he will use his magician's power to shake them with the thunders and blast them with the lightnings of all Printing-House Square.

Distinguished as a scholar, statesman, diplomatist, philosopher, and man of science—foremost of all as a printer—it is fitting that statues should be erected all over our land in honor of the memory of Franklin; and having dipped his first tallow-candle in Boston, there is peculiar propriety in his being so honored there; but from its position as the metropolitan city of America, there is no place more fitting than the City of New York; and, as the local point from which radiate the "thoughts that breathe and the words that burn," borne by the resistless steam-charger or sped by the lightning which he first tamed, Printing-House Square is of all places the most fitting for a memorial of the statesman, philosopher, and printer. There may it long stand, a reminder of the generations past and an exemplar for the ages to come.

Mr. Hill favored the company with appropriate songs at suitable intervals. They were given in a fine voice and with much taste and feeling. Encores were repeatedly demanded.

Volunteer toasts and sentiments having been requested, Mr. Douglas Taylor, then presiding, read the following, and called upon Mr. Thomas N. Rooker, of the New York Tribune, for a response.

THE KITE, THE KEY, AND THE TELEGRAPH. *While the Kite beguiled the Clouds, the Key unlocked the Starry Mansion, and Franklin, with a string, led Jove's eldest daughter to the altar of Science, where she was wedded by Morse to the Telegraph. The happy couple are now spending their Honeymoon—spangling the Earth with the jewels of Civilization.*

Mr. Rooker was greeted with repeated cheers. When silence was called, he said:

Mr. Chairman, Ladies and Fellow-Craftsmen:

I have been asked to make a speech. I am a type-setter, and as a rule, a type-setter prefers to allow his work to speak for itself, for the reason that types sometimes tell lies, or at least make white appear black —something like a well-developed case of small-pox—when the truth, if spoken, would give white a rosy, pleasant hue. In addition to this, he has no choice of the words that are selected for the lips of the types, and they sometimes help to hoist a very large man on top of a very small apex, leaving him a very limited field for action; or, *vice versa*, they put a very small man in a large field, and he is lost sight of—as the Babes in the Woods were. As I am forbid by my conscience from making a speech, I will tell you a legend, which, though it be "a thrice told tale," vexing your drowsy ears, is nevertheless worthy of your listening and remembrance—especially as it has been alluded to by many distinguished persons here present. In fact, it is undoubtedly being spoken of by many who are not present this evening—people in other countries. The fishes in the sea are opening and shutting their eyes and ears, if they have "ears to hear;" if not, their eyes and gills. Gills they have, I know, for I have caught fish, and I have seen their gills. I say that the fishes in the sea are opening and shutting their eyes and ears—or gills, if more correct—listening to the legend as it flashes over the cable. The tale I propose to recite I shall call "The Runaway Match," because there was a great deal of love in it, which resulted in a wedding, a grand bridal tour, and a happy honeymoon. Without further delay I shall commence the story, because I have bad copy and solid matter—that is, my memory is bad, and my words so closely packed in my throat that my tongue cannot sort them quickly—and I want to get rid of it, in order that I may get a "fat-take," which I see before me.

Once on a time there lived a powerful and bad king in a rich and beautiful country, and he had many bad men in his Council of State, and these bad men were constantly urging him to oppress his subjects with taxes on their labor, and he refused to allow them to worship God as seemed to them meet and proper, in order that he and they might carouse as bacchanalians. In other words, they "put on the livery of heaven to serve the devil in." After many years of suffering, a few of his people determined to leave the land of their birth and seek better fortune—and freedom to worship God. This small band of God-fearing and God-loving men and women embarked on board ship and sailed forth over the sea, with God's breath in their sails and God's loving eyes at the helm. When they sighted land, on "New England's rock-bound coast," their hearts were impregnated with holy thanks, and their eyes floated in a flood of tears born of joy and gladness. I will not detain you by telling how soft and pleasant, and yet so firm, Plymouth Rock felt beneath their feet. Plymouth Rock, itself, may tell you that, and although others have done as I propose to do, and allowed Plymouth Rock to tell its story until its tongue, like the Blarney Stone of Ireland, is nearly worn out, still, Mr. Chairman, any one can hear it speak, like an old and honored veteran, whether that one be curious about the statesman or the soldier who came in after time from those whose feet pressed its grand, rugged bosom. The people I am talking about had school-houses in their brains, churches in their hearts, and God in their souls. The school-houses and the churches brought forth of their kind to such an extent that it is possible for a man to stand and reach out his hands to the door of the one and to the pulpit of the other, this blessed land over—and so be it evermore.

Time, like a jack-knife, wears away by use, and it is how it is used, whether it is well worn out or not. We will suppose that Time was well used, and in after years an industrious and frugal family, as well bred and educated as their opportunity and means permitted—whose surname was Franklin—lived in Boston. Ladies, this was many years ago—possibly before you were born; for ladies, I believe, are never old; but some of you may have heard of Boston—it is called, sometimes, the "Hub of the Universe"—and then, again, Boston is quite noted for a Tea Party, which the old—old, did I say?—I mean which the young ladies assisted in getting up. Well, the head of this family of Franklins was a soap and candle maker, and, in his trade, honest and famous. He had a boy named Benjamin; but then, as now, called Ben; because Ben is quicker said than Benjamin, and the people at that time saved their breath to cool their porridge. Ben was set at work in his father's chandlery; but dipping candles and boiling soap neither satisfied his ambition nor gratified his olfactory nerves. The consequence of which was that he left, and went into his brother's printing-office. Ben liked to read books, and his memory served him faithfully—it kept the truths he read firmly in its grasp, and it shook the chaff off as a fan-mill cleans grain. The pure grain fed and nurtured his mind until it became strong and powerful, as well as wise and brilliant.

At this time there was another family, then and since quite famous, by the name of Civilization. Some of its children had traveled and been wrecked in distant countries, but in this country it had prospered, and had grown very popular and influential. The eldest son was a beautiful, manly-looking young man, and as his parents were rich and nobly proud, he had received the best education that money could procure for him. He was, truly, well educated, for he took learning as readily as children take milk. His beauty of form and person, his courteous manners, and his pleasant, sympathetic voice, made him the envy of his associates, because the girls took to him; and no party, dance, or singing-school was complete without his presence. But he, like Ben, was not content with common things—his ambition pointed higher. He would have none other than a goddess for his wife. How to get her was the cross he bore. One day Ben met him wandering through the streets and lanes of the city, sad and low spirited, and he at once asked his friend why he was so sad and down-hearted. He soon learned that a shaft from Cupid's bow had pierced his heart. His dream had been gratified—he had seen Lightning, the beautiful daughter of Jove, when taking her evening ramble, attended by her maids of honor, the Pleiades. From that moment until he met Ben, he was as unhappy a swain as Poet ever sang about. When Ben had heard his story, he pitied him, and promised to be his friend. He told him how many had tried to get her—how closely Jove watched her, and how he raved and roared whenever she went for an airing; that this raving and roaring frightened many wise and good people, and, the consequence would be, that unless she was allowed to receive company and select a mate, she would become an old maid, which was a great sin in either mortal or immortal; and that he was determined to outwit the old chap whenever he found a person who was worthy of her—one who would love and cherish her as she deserved. If his friend really possessed the divine afflatus, he would assist him in obtaining the being who alone could make him happy and prosperous. Now, Lightning had seen young Civilization, and in her heart had said, "Would 'that Heaven had made her such a man.'" In truth, she was as deeply in love as he. Where two agree, a bargain is soon made. "But, Ben," said young Civilization, "how am I to get her from her home? Jove, you say, watches with sleepless eyes her every movement. What shall I do?" "Do?" said Ben, "why, my boy, do nothing. Leave the doing of things to me. Go, see the Priest, and arrange for the wedding ceremony. I will be with you shortly."

Ben went home and made a kite, took a ball of twine, a key, and a bottle, and then went out into a field. There was a brisk breeze, the clouds were low and heavy, and up went the kite. The key was arranged, and the bottle placed so as to catch any messenger Jove might send for his daughter. Now commenced trembling Anxiety her brief life. I can see in my mind's eye the waltzing, chasseing, bowing, coquetting kite, as she swings her tail about—in the manner that a proud dame sweeps her train. "Set a thief to catch a thief" is an old and wise saying. So Ben thought when he decided to send a coquette to catch a coquette—for he believed then that Miss Lightning was nothing but a coquette, who was fond of flashing in the air. But he was mistaken, as men before and after him have been. She was a faithful, bright, and brilliant woman. She was a warm-hearted, industrious and trustworthy one—as the legend shows. The kite was equally trustworthy, for it beguiled the clouds so admirably that Jove himself became amazed, and while he and his retinue were watching the sport, Ben unlocked the Starry Mansion and out stepped the future Bride, whom he led by a string to the Earth. Jove, seeing what had been done, sent Taurus to gore the thief, and to bring Lightning back—as grandly as John Alden took Priscilla to his home. It was of no use—Ben was too good a Bull-fighter. He bottled him, and he kept him. And, friends, perhaps this may account for the fact that men, even at this late day, often get tossed when they pull a cork from a bottle. Taurus, I have heard, does sometimes get loose in Wall street, and then he sets "things kiting."

Ben and the Bride set off in search of young Civilization, whom they found talking to the Priest who was to make them bone of one bone and flesh of one flesh. This Priest had become very celebrated in consequence of a curious invention which he called a Telegraph. He was a learned man, and he took two Greek words and made one English word, signifying, Webster says, "far, far off" and "to write." The Poet has expressed the idea better, I think, when he says "thou art so near and yet so far." Before he had invented this wonder, he had been a poor artist. I don't mean that he was a poor painter, but that he worked hard and faithfully, and remained a poor man—similar to many of my friends. I have no hesitation in saying, however, that his practice in making straight and curved lines, when an artist, was of great use to him when he commenced putting up his poles for the Telegraph, for you know that there are several straight and curved-line Telegraph Companies in the world. In fact, it was necessary that there should be straight and curved lines, for from the North to the South Poles the lines are very nearly straight, and around the world one has to go in a circle, as Andy Johnson, when he made his celebrated tour. He went "Bobbing Round." When all things were well and fitly done—the Bonds of Matrimony drawn up and signed in presence of friends—the party went to the altar of Science, and there before God and man the twain were made one.

Flags flouted the wind; cannon roared with delight, and the sun gilded the roof of the poor man's cottage as gorgeously as he blazed in the windows of the palace. Soon after, the happy pair stepped into their chariot for their Bridal tour. The old shoes which were thrown after them, as they left the station, if gathered, would have made a monument as large as the one on Bunker Hill, and it would have been as enduring as the pyramids. Let me say, friends, that although many were shoeless, none were soulless. Possibly it was this event which suggested the invention of the shoemaking machines, which are "pegging away" so lively in the New England States. When last heard from, this happy couple were spending their honeymoon traveling round the world—spangling the Earth with the rich jewels of Civilization. God grant that their honeymoon may outlast the Centuries.

Mr. Chairman, I have told you the legend of the "Runaway Match." I ask in return that you sanction my request to the ladies who have so attentively listened, that they join me, you, and my craftsmen in drinking to "The Kite, the Key, and the Telegraph." To do this we will uncork the bottle, and let Taurus roar and toss us up into the seventh heaven.

At midnight the exercises were closed, and the company separated. Every participant who had been in the habit of attending public dinners volunteered the remark that the Franklin Banquet had been the most successful dinner of the season.

IX

The Comments of the Press.

[From the New York Tribune, Jan. 24, 1872.]

THE FRANKLIN STATUE.

WHEN, last week, the enveloping banners were removed and the Statue of Franklin was disclosed, there was a moment of genuine and hearty applause. Among the majority this was, of course, because the bronze was fresh and shining, and the well-known face and figure came suddenly out of their brilliant covering like those of an old friend. But even among the judicious minority there was something of a feeling of positive relief as the veil fell and they knew the worst. There has been so much of charlatanism in the recent contracts for works of art, that the public naturally expect that the unveiling of a statue will be a disclosure almost as horrible as that of the mysterious Prophet of Khorassan. To be entirely candid, there was very little to be expected of this long-heralded bronze, and therefore the satisfaction of every one was so much the greater, that it turned out to be a most respectable statue. The press, thoroughly appreciating the generosity and public spirit of the donor, were prepared to be as lenient as possible in criticism, and for that reason it is the more gratifying that there is no especial demand for lenity. It is a rather conventional statue, made in a workmanlike manner, with a close adherence to historical truth. The likeness is well caught, and though it is not the great Franklin of the best French portraits, it is a fair enough copy of the every-day sage and philosopher of common life. The attitude is easy and natural, though, like many other works of the kind, it has its better and worse side. Viewed from the north, it is rather lacking in dignity. The outstretched arm is deficient in firmness of purpose, and the whole figure seems neither speaking nor silent. But from the east, that is to say, standing on the left hand of the Statue, it creates a most agreeable and harmonious impression. The tall stature of the President of Pennsylvania is seen in its just proportions, for, though Thackeray, in the Virginians, speaks of him as "the little postmaster," he was 5 feet 10½ inches high. The paper in his left hand and the argumentative *pose* of the right fall into their proper relation. The head of Franklin, one of the grandest known to art or history, is always a godsend to the sculptor, and in this case it had not been wronged in the handling. The long, wavy hair, which in defiance of the stiff and artificial mode of the day, Franklin wore when presented at Versailles, falls back from the placid, gravely smiling face, and gives to the superb head a character which is superior to changing styles or fashions. On the whole, it is a creditable statue, and an ornament to Printing-House Square. It is well placed and well framed, with the City Hall Park in front and the newspaper offices of the present and future behind it.

[From the New York Tribune, January 17, 1872.]

FRANKLIN.

While the crowd gathers, this morning, about the Statue beneath our windows, in Printing-House Square, it is worth while to turn back for a moment to the character of the man whom it commemorates.

It is the greatest reputations alone which increase with passing years. It is only the sterling and efficient characters that have influenced the course of civilization who require distance for their full appreciation. What Landor said of Shakespeare is applicable to them; the concurring verdict of successive generations stands as the agreement of individuals. We are too young a nation to count many of these sure immortalities. But one of the most unquestionable is certainly the philosopher and statesman whom his fellow-craftsmen agree to honor to-day.

No figure of our great revolutionary epoch has gained more in dignity and importance since those days. The cloud of calumny and detraction which pursued him so vindictively in life has entirely passed away in the light of authentic history. All there was of doubtful or questionable in the record of his acts has been cleared off by the pens of investigators like Parton and Loménie, Bancroft and Bigelow. At each addition which is made to the history of the process by which we became a nation, the part he bore in the great work becomes more clearly revealed and gains in significance. Every advance which is made in material science bears witness to the wisdom and sagacity of that self-taught savant whose robust common sense grappled successfully with the most intricate problems of nature. His contributions to the science of government are even to-day well worthy the best consideration of statesmen. The whole world is enjoying to-day the practical results of his scientific insight and labor, and even the crowning glory of the telegraph was withheld from his ardent research and given to Morse only because the world was not ready for it a generation ago. When we see the marvelously accurate approaches which he made to that miracle of science, we can fancy the hand of Providence laid upon the eager eyes which were about to surprise the secret of the next century.

So many-sided was this wholesome genius that there seem to be many Franklins in the world's memory. There is a scholar whose work is co-extensive with civilization. There is a statesman whose hand is seen in the firm foundations of the great Republic. There is a diplomatist who achieved the most important results ever accomplished since heralds went on embassies. There is a homely philosopher and moralist whose simple and chatty counsels are the daily gospel of thousands of firesides. Yet it is not a character of contrasts or surprises. In its rounded symmetry we see the natural development of a great intellect guided and controlled by great goodness. He was a skillful and industrious workman; and so gained means and leisure to devote himself to science and politics. It was a favorite saying of his father in the old candle-shop at Boston, "Seest thou a man diligent in business, he shall stand before kings." No man ever lived more diligent in business, and no man ever stood with more of the dignity of upright manhood before kings.

He has passed into a type of democracy here and abroad. At home his name indicates thrift, intelligence, integrity, and love of country, the qualities which save Republics. Abroad he is our best known if not our greatest name. His serene and noble countenance is as familiar in Europe as that of any monarch. After sustaining in England the cause of the Colonies against the aggressions of George III., he went to France to enlist the assistance of a dying despotism in favor of the new-born democracy. Arriving in a time of moral and political chaos, when the old system was passing away and no man knew it, he became at once the point of attraction for all the wavering and stormy currents of thought and inquiry. He was a light shining in darkness, and though the darkness comprehended not, it became filled with a strange restlessness and excitement. The moths of the court flew to the new light. They petted and flattered him; they made democracy fashionable at

Versailles. When Joseph II. of Austria came down to Paris to visit his sister, Marie Antoinette, he shook his head over this ominous popularity of the Republican philosopher, and said: "Madame, the trade we live by is that of Royalists." But as long as Franklin stayed, this unconscious homage of the past to the future continued, and when he went home he received an almost royal farewell. They have never forgotten him. To this hour the most popular memory of a foreigner in France is that of Franklin. Again in our day we see a despotism flattering democracy in his name. One of the new boulevards of the Trocadero, opened for the Exposition of 1867, is called the Avenue Franklin.

To-day he receives a fitting and impressive recognition at the hands of the craft to which he belonged, and on which he conferred unquestioned honor. However the rest of the world may have distinguished and glorified him, this tribute has still its own full and novel significance. Philadelphia has his grave, and Boston has set up his statue in commemoration of his nativity. But it is especially becoming that here, in the first city of the continent, his image should stand, surrounded on every side by the engines of that mighty power whose importance he was the first to appreciate and acknowledge. The intervention of saints and the worship of ancestors have place in most of the religions of the globe. It will do the Press of America no harm to have always before them, in the very center of their highest activity, the face and form of our first and greatest printer and editor, recalling continually the needed lesson that thrift is not greed or meanness, that politics nobly pursued are ennobling, that the first obligation of Science is to better the condition of humanity, and that the surest road of intelligence to fortune and to enduring fame is that of industry and integrity and patriotism.

[From the New York World, January 17, 1872.]

FRANKLIN AND WASHINGTON.

To-day, in one of the busiest thoroughfares of New York, amidst the creations and monuments, such as a century ago were not dreamed of, of the art of which in America Franklin may be called the founder, is to be unveiled a memorial, the moral of which it may be well to state, familiar as the story is. It is the statue of one of the two Americans of ancient days who, utterly unlike in character and temper, morally and intellectually, stand, in the estimation of the world, "a head and shoulders taller" than all else. Washington was the incarnation of the high-toned cavalier—dignified in bearing as in sentiment, austere, chivalric. If there were cracks and minute fissures in his moral crystal, they did not disfigure the bright, colorless surface, and had to be looked at closely to be discovered at all. Franklin was, if not exactly the reverse, not far from it. He was the reality of the spirit of his native soil, purged of Puritan asceticism. Of a large brain and a susceptible nature, which showed itself, according to all concurrent testimony, in the most courteous manners, he was still, from first to last, the true, politic, money-loving, worldly-wise New Englander. None the worse for that. He was a man of lower motives than Washington, and, as we all know (and to do him full justice he was no hypocrite), of far less decorous morals. We are not going to say he was none the worse for that; but we do say there was a manliness about Franklin's weaknesses in these respects that disarms censure. There was one intellectual difference between them which is very marked. Neither were men of early education or scholarship, and to the day of his death Washington was never able to free himself from the effects of want of early culture. Franklin had within him the great instincts of literary motive, and became by the mere effort of his own will—by intellectual processes that are simply marvelous—the best writer of his time on this side of the Atlantic. In one respect—and here let the parallel close—they were the same. If ever men were true lovers of their native soil—persevering assertors of its rights as peaceful colonies, and as States warring in all the uncertainty of initiate independence, or, having secured it, striving to preserve and consolidate it—they were. There was no faltering; and censorious history—that which libelers of the dead have written and will continue to write—has never been able to hint a doubt or whisper distrust.

Who, then, better deserves a memorial monument than this one of the two, and where can it be better placed than in the crowded and strictly professional vicinage which to-day will gaze upon it? The equestrian Washington, with imperial mien and outstretched arm, like the Aurelian figure of the Capitol, is not more in his place on the spot consecrated to Union than will be homely, practical Benjamin Franklin in the modest nook of Printing-House Square. And who more appropriately to unveil the figure than he, our venerable townsman, who, grasping the magnetic fire in his hand, has sent it round the earth to do his bidding? Nor, in the professional sympathy which the occasion excites, should we pass unnoticed the gracefulness of the selection which is made for the orator of the occasion of that veteran of the press, whose lot is cast in quieter times, who, like Franklin, has made himself what he is, and who, it is no flattery to say, writes as vigorous English as ever Franklin did.

It is almost an insult to our readers to recapitulate the story of the eighty-four years of this wonderful career. Nor shall we attempt to do it. It nearly fills up the century, with the small margin of sixteen years—six at the beginning and ten at the end. Regarding them carelessly as contemporaneous, we are apt to forget that Franklin was twenty-six years of age and had, locally at least, made his mark when Washington was born. When they were first brought in contact on the Braddock campaign of 1755, the young soldier was twenty-three and the printer and postmaster a man of nearly fifty. And this prompts a suggestion with reference to the Franklin career which is often lost sight of, and which to-day may be appropriately recalled, at least for the consolation of those who fancy their careers of usefulness ended. It is something like Michael Angelo at seventy-one undertaking St. Peter's. When Franklin contemplated returning from England on his second visit, in 1766, he expressed great doubt as to his ability to survive the voyage, and his belief that his day of work was over. Yet after that, what did not this marvelous "old man" live to see and do? He crossed the Atlantic no less than three times; he saw a civil war break out and terminate; he heard independence declared and acknowledged; he framed the first Constitution of Pennsylvania and was Governor under it; he negotiated the alliance with France; he signed the definitive treaty of peace with Great Britain; he lived to have the dream of 1754 realized in 1787 and Federal institutions created, and was a member of the august body which framed the Constitution of the Union. All this he did after he had condemned himself as too old and feeble to work at all!

But to return for a moment to those features of Franklin's career, aside from such as were political, which strengthen his claim on the gratitude of mankind. There was in all the phases of his moral and intellectual nature the most perfect self-reliance and yet the most unaffected humility. He never boasts. When, in 1755, as we have said, he went to Annapolis as colonial postmaster—"little Mr. Franklin," as the author of the "Virginians" calls him—to confer with Braddock and co-operate with young Major Washington, little cared the colonial world or the world at large of the marvelous scientific discovery he had made three years before in the garden at Philadelphia, in the identification of the elemental lightning of the atmosphere with the common hand-made electricity of the machine. "Next to the discovery of gravitation," says a modern

English writer, "this is the most remarkable fetch of remote identification which the history of science presents." It was a secret which had remained hidden beyond the reach of the deepest plummet that ancient or modern intelligence had dropped from the days when Aristotle observed the attraction and repulsion of vitreous substances and the sparks from the human hair. It was for our forest-born philosopher to conceive the idea, and by cool, cautious ratiocination, such as belonged to his nature, to demonstrate it. "Only," says the same author we have quoted, "a cool, intellectual nature such as distinguished Franklin was a match for a case like this. He could face the evolution of a thunder-storm, and watch it with all the calmness that he would have shown in an ordinary philosophical experiment, deliberately bethinking himself the while of any parallel phenomenon wherewith to identify and illustrate it." So grand, so intellectually and morally sublime, as we meditate on it, does this dealing with nature's secrets seem, that we are conscious of something kindred to regret that such a genius should have had any contact with the petty doings of petty men—with politics, with statesmanship—even though it were for the sake of human liberty and the destinies of a nascent nation. The "tyrant's sceptre" is a poor trophy alongside of "heaven's lightning."

This perhaps is, and certainly may be called, "sentimentalism;" but it rises to the lips involuntarily and is entirely consistent with strenuous admiration of Franklin's public and political achievements. There is one portion of the latter to which full justice can never be done. We refer to his services in France from December, 1776—for he arrived there just as Washington, in despair, was flying across New Jersey—till the peace of 1783. Reader of our story, if you wish to know to whom, under Providence and next to Washington, to owe gratitude for success in those dark hours of agony, study what Franklin did and suffered! Then was it that his common sense asserted itself. It is a curious and a tangled record, of which this may be safely said, that if America's diplomacy had been in the uncontrolled hands of Franklin's eminent but crotchety colleagues, very different would have been the result. John Adams's Puritan perversity (perfectly honest and patriotic) and Mr. Jay's austere, Huguenot impracticability were enough to shipwreck anything. But the serene, practical wisdom of Franklin controlled the "rough-hewing" of his impulsive colleagues, and the *entente cordiale*, literally, was maintained, and Rochambeau was at Yorktown and Vergennes was loyal to the end.

It was on his return from the doing of this great work that, on the 14th of September, 1785, the old man of seventy-nine made this entry in his diary: "With the flood-tide in the morning came a light breeze, which brought us above Gloucester Point, and then we saw 'dear Philadelphia.'" And Philadelphia, his first haven of rest when he fled in natural discontent from Boston, was very dear to him. There he had gained fame, and there he had strenuously done good. Hardly an institution of learning or charity in that great community but on its foundation stone the name of Franklin is not carved. There fifty-seven years of his life were passed. There, in the fullness, almost the superfluity of years, he died; and there, honored in every relation of life, his descendants live; and yet—we say it with pride—New York first builds what may be termed a public statute to his memory. Perhaps we are not strictly accurate in this. There are two statues erected by private munificence in Philadelphia—one over the library which he founded, and one in an inconvenient and perilous attitude out of the window of a newspaper office; and Boston, in honor of his early flight, has her statue too. But the impulse of New York to do this memorial honor, at the end of a hundred and sixty-six years, is a purely metropolitan one. It is to do honor to the man of America. Franklin's contact with New York was a very slight one. On the 23d of October, 1723, more than a century and a-half ago, Benjamin Franklin, runaway apprentice, landed at one of the poor, rickety slips on the East River, and after a pause in the poor village, hastened onward, foot-sore and weary, across the sands and swamps of New Jersey. He was no doubt here on his way to the Albany Colonial Convention of 1754, and again when, in the spring of 1776, he came to have an interview with his old friend Lord Howe, on Staten Island. This is all the personal contact we can trace.

But what of that? What if it were less? New York to-day honors the man of history!

[From the Commercial Advertiser, January 17, 1872.]

THE EXAMPLE OF FRANKLIN.

This is no monument or statue-erecting age, as the long drawn out failures to commemorate the departed great, by a resort to popular subscription, most plainly show. If the monumental marble is to rise, the impulse must come from private enterprise or legislative appropriation.

Hence it happens that many men, who have a high place in the public appreciation, are without the statues and monuments which are forever being proposed for them. In the olden time, warriors and statesmen were at once put into brass; later, these effigies appeared on a swinging tavern sign; now they give name to restaurants and saloons, to hotels and conspicuous buildings, to banks and insurance companies, to streets and steamboats. In some way they are commemorated and so they never go out of the common speech of the people. New York has many suitable places for statues, and there are many noble characters to distinguish in this way. But, so far, very few of them have been so honored. To-day, however, the City turns aside from its busy life to honor the memory of one who stands forth in the national history as the completest type of many of the best qualities which have vitalized American character, and given wealth, prosperity, and progress to this land. Good sense, thrift, earnestness, frankness, honesty, self-confidence, simplicity, determination, were the leading characteristics of Benjamin Franklin, who bore no second part in assuring our National Independence, and whose name and features are as familiar to Europe as those of Washington himself. The life of Franklin measured the better part of a century. He was born in 1706 and died in 1790. His nurture was in the Colonies, which he saw pass through the French War and the War of Independence. He founded a University, he gave position and dignity to the Press. As one of the framers of the Immortal Declaration, he gave a charter of liberty to the struggling and oppressed of all ages and climes. As the compiler of an almanac, he furnished the poor and lowly, the thrifty and industrious, with the wisest saws, and maxims most encouraging to virtue and prosperity. Long before the Revolution, he invented the lightning rod and the stove which bears his name. He was ever a restless promoter of municipal reform. He improved the city watch of Philadelphia, and established its first fire company. He held numerous offices, and in all he magnified his place and made it a centre of improvement and progress. He was Postmaster-general for America in 1753, and as such took part in the fitting out of Braddock's expedition. He became a soldier himself, and narrowly escaped being made a General—this appointment he modestly declined. English and Continental Universities showered their honors upon him. He stood before Kings, and in Courts where he was insulted and maligned. But his grave and dignified demeanor, his plain garb, his fascinating conversation, and his lofty love of truth and of freedom won him many friends, and gave credit and respect to the cause he advocated. It was after Franklin had attained the age of three-score that he accomplished the greatest political results of his life. He felt that he was too old for the work assigned him, and asked to be excused. But his country could not spare him, and it was in his later years that he achieved the triumphs by which he won the chief place in the affections of his countrymen. As our negotiator abroad, and a framer of the Constitution at home, Franklin crowned the labors of his illustrious career, and merited no second place in the National Pantheon. His well-known figure now confronts the public gaze in one of the busiest squares of the metropolis, and in the very midst of the machinery of intelligence he so well knew how to use, when that machinery was in its rudest form. His mild and thoughtful face will teach the lesson that all New York may learn daily with profit—the lesson which Franklin says was his constant rule—"To go straight forward in doing what appears to me to be right, leaving the consequences to Providence." In the hurried rush of the present, this example of integrity, purity, patriotism, honor, and thrift may be profitably recalled.

[From the New York Evening Mail, January 17, 1872.]

FRANKLIN.

In the month of October, 1723, after a three days' passage from Boston, a young runaway apprentice boy arrived in this city with no more worldly effects than he could easily carry in his hand. He was looking for employment in the only trade of which he had any knowledge, that of printing. His anxious search was entirely in vain, for the reason that the little Dutch provincial City of New York had at that time not a single newspaper office, and the only job office there was here had no work for him to do. Had such a harbor been open to receive the adventurous and stout-hearted young printer-boy, in all human probability New York would to-day enjoy the proud distinction, which is the boast of Philadelphia, of being "the city of Franklin."

To-day, however, in one of the busiest quarters of the metropolis, and in the centre of a square whose name suggests its actual surroundings, the successors to the printer's apprentice of 1723 have assembled to dedicate a bronze statue in his honor. Within a few hundred feet of this statue are scores of printing presses whose marvelous capacity for multiplying newspapers would astonish Franklin quite as much as the practical applications of his discovering that electricity might be made subject to human control. Among the speakers who have been called on to assist in the honors of the day, is the man who has justified his proud title of "Our later Franklin," by a career equally notable and more wholly devoted to the profession which the early philosopher and statesman largely neglected in his later years. To-day and this evening the brightest lights of our newspaper fraternity will unite in paying homage to their sensible, sagacious and practical Patron Saint, and within twenty-four hours, by the magic of electricity and the types, a whole Continent will be able to join in sympathy with this demonstration here to-day.

We shall not attempt either a criticism or an eulogium upon Franklin. No one of our early great men is more thoroughly understood. He was frank and truthful and strong enough to portray his own weaknesses and faults, and comes down to us as a real presence. Some of his most famous contemporaries have been so unreservedly eulogized that they have become like the mythical heroes of Greece and Rome. Franklin we know. A broad, genial, many-sided man, he appeals to the common sense of practical farmers and business men, while the statesman and the scientific student find in him the rarest combination of insight, keenness of observation, faultless logic and capacity for wide generalization. The youngest boy will read his autobiography with as keen zest as a novel. The wisest man will find the same frank story full of instruction.

The permanence, universality and growth of Franklin's fame have not been the result of chance. It has been the legitimate triumph of one of the most genuine characters ever developed. There have been greater philosophers, but what one of them has made his genius so useful to the race? Other men did more to shape the legislative policy of the young Republic, but who contributed so much towards the education of the colonies that fitted them for independence or towards securing foreign aid in our time of trial? Other great men have admitted their errors of life and continued to commit them. Franklin profited by his own mistakes and set a helpful example. He was unconsciously the most efficient advocate of democracy by the simple grandeur of his career, which made the plain American diplomat, at the most artificial Court in Europe, the acknowledged peer of the highest and courted of all. He stood there for the unadorned and untitled dignity of human nature, and every homage paid to him was a compliment to humanity itself.

Mr. Parton says that the great lesson of Franklin's life to all cultivated men was: "*Communicate*." This lesson will not be lost to-day on the hundreds of those whose daily business it is to follow humbly after Franklin's example. If all of Franklin's journalistic successors here will study his career more faithfully by reason of this fresh ceremonial in his honor, the day will not have been wasted. Let them learn to imitate his patience, his charity, his willingness to be convinced, his unceasing efforts to popularize great truths, his industry, his freedom from opinionativeness, and his breadth of view.

[From the Brooklyn Union, January 17, 1872.]

THE FRANKLIN STATUE.

To-day, the fraternities of journalists and printers in the Empire City of the New World are to be publicly—honored were going to write, but that is not the proper word—reprimanded, is the better term. Yes, the editors and printers of the American metropolis are to be generously reprimanded by Captain Albert De Groot, a retired steamboat navigator, who, seeing that they have neglected to erect any kind of a public testimonial in honor of the one member of their craft who, above all others, honored them by his labors, has placed at his own cost and presented to them an imposing statue of Franklin in the most conspicuous position in the city. The circumstance is altogether a very remarkable one, and it should be properly commemorated. Philadelphia and Boston long since erected statues and other monumental testimonials of their regard for the memory of Franklin, but in New York nothing of the kind has been done, with the exception of bestowing his name upon one small, triangular "square," and upon one street. The great publishing house in Franklin square have placed an iron statue of Franklin in a niche of their vast building, but that can hardly be called a public testimonial. The elemosynary statute of Captain De Groot has been placed on a temporary pedestal in what is called Printing-House Square, in front of the publication offices of the Times, the Tribune, and the Sun. The locality was well chosen, and, if the statue be worthy of the man in whose honor it has been erected, it will be a public benefit; but if it should prove deficient in the artistic excellence which the æsthetic education of the age demands, it will be an eye-sore, an annoyance, and a disgrace. Statues being in themselves the most useless of all the creations of human industry, can only be justified by their excellence as works of art. Unless they are so superlatively good as to afford pleasure to those who idly gaze upon them, they are a standing insult to the memories they are intended to honor, and a reproach to those who erect them. We trust that the De Groot Statue will prove all that it should be, and that when it is unveiled to the crowd to-day, it may be received with the honest cheers of grateful enthusiasts in art. But, let the work be what it may, we are bound to honor the generous motives of its liberal donor.

Franklin, above all other men of his age, or, indeed, of any age, stands least in need of extraneous memorials to keep his name prominent before the world. He is pre-eminently the great man of America, and was indebted to no accident for his greatness. Washington would have been unknown but for the Revolution. He would not have been distinguished beyond many other Virginia gentlemen who cultivated their plantations on the Potomac. But the adventurous printer's apprentice from Boston had gained a world-wide renown long before he gave the influence of his great name and the fruits of his industrious life to inaugurate and sustain the cause which the genius of Washington rendered successful. Looking now at all the facts of our Revolutionary struggle it is difficult to see how the triumphant end could have been attained without the assistance rendered by Franklin. Of no other man, except Washington, could so much be said.

It has became common of late years, among the Bohemians of literature, to speak slightly or to sneer at the name of Franklin, on the ground of the prudential maxims which he published in his "Poor Richard's Almanac." But apart from the literary merit of those immortal maxims—their wit and humor—they have proved to this country a surer source of wealth and happiness than the gold gulches of California. They were showered upon the country just at the time when the national mind was being moulded into a permanent form; when the diverse elements of our population were in the process of amalgamating into a concrete character, and, above all other men, Franklin has the best right to be called the Father of his Country. There is no special reason why New York, more than any other town in the United States, should erect a monument in honor of Franklin, for his local connection with the city was purely accidental. He merely passed through New York, like any other traveler. He landed at Peck Slip, on the East River, in October, 1723, when he was drifting towards Philadelphia; and he sailed from New York, when he went, at the age of forty, to represent the colonies of Pennsylvania, New Jersey, and New York before King George the III.;

but New York, as the metropolis of the Union, is bound in its monumental structures, after it shall have honored the memories of its local worthies who deserve such honors, to erect a suitable testimonial to express the gratitude of its people for the inestimable benefits derived from the labors and the example of the great patriot and philosopher, Franklin.

Appendix.

[From the Printers' Circular.]

HOW THE STATUE CAME TO BE ERECTED.

Knowing that Mr. Peter C. Baker, of New York city, had been identified with the movement in favor of the Franklin Statue, from its inception to its completion, we wrote to him for the particulars, and more especially as to who was the first to suggest it. His answer is so full of interesting details, that we think our readers will thank us for publishing it entire. We therefore conclude by giving the

LETTER FROM MR. PETER C. BAKER.

New York, January 23, 1872.

To the Editor of the Printers' Circular:

I feel complimented by your letter, for it assures me that you know something of the connection I have had with our Franklin Statue. Captain De Groot, in his modest little speech at the banquet, told all of the story I cared to have named. He said it was at "Mr. Baker's suggestion" that he was induced to enter upon the enterprise. The truth is, that, for many years, I had in my mind the idea of a Franklin Statue for the city of New York, and I could think of no place quite so appropriate as Printing-House Square, on whose front, and in whose immediate neighborhood, so large a proportion of the great newspapers and printing-houses stand. All now admit that this is the most appropriate place for the Franklin Statue. I always knew that, and I was determined that, sooner or later, "Old Ben" should smile upon us. One day, when Captain De Groot was in our office, now nearly two years ago, he spoke of his labors and success connected with carrying through the "Vanderbilt Bronzes." After he had concluded, I took him to the front window, and pointed to the open space in front of the Times and Tribune buildings. I said, "Captain, I have long had in my mind that we must have a statue of Franklin standing on that spot, and I hope to live long enough to see one just there." He looked at me for a moment, and replied, "Would you really like to see Franklin's statue there?" "Yes," I said, "and I am determined to have one there if I live long enough." "You shall have it!" he said. "The idea strikes me as good, and the Press has done so much for me in my various public positions that I feel just like making a statue, and presenting it to the Press and the Printers. I will do it! You shall have it!" he insisted. I confess that I could hardly believe he was in earnest; for I knew how great the cost would be. But the Captain insisted that he meant just what he said; and, to prove his sincerity, he promised to bring a small model, or "statuette," in a few days. And he did. We exhibited this small figure in our office for several days—sending out notices to literary and artistic gentlemen, who came and generally expressed themselves pleased with the design.

Then De Groot began work in earnest. He employed Ernst Plassman, a German sculptor of our city, to make a colossal figure in clay. Plassman gathered about him all the Franklin busts, and portraits, and costumes he could find, and labored conscientiously for several months to make a figure worthy of the great Printer and Philosopher. When he had completed his work in plaster, we sent out invitations to a large number of gentlemen connected with the Press, and identified with Art, requesting them to visit Plassman's rooms, and express their opinion of his work. The Statue was left standing for such inspection several weeks. Many good suggestions were made; and finally, although the figure was a fine one, and met with general approval, Plassman said, "I can do better—I will make another." And he broke up the first model, and began another. After several months, the second figure was completed. Again we sent out invitations to the same class of gentlemen as at first. Quite a large number came to see the revised model, and nearly all were pleased with the figure. I was accustomed to go every morning, for a good while, to hear what was said. I felt, in a certain sense, responsible for the truthfulness of the statue, and was determined that only a creditable work of art should be placed in Printing-House Square. I may fairly say that some important changes were made by my direction. And the face was made more like Franklin's by my persistent efforts to have the sculptor change and change till it suited me.

But I must stop. The rest is soon told. The bronze founders were extremely successful, and the filers and the finishers who came after, did their best, and did well. "So all the people say." You must come on and judge for yourself. We all feel that we have a noble statue—worthy of Franklin, worthy of our city, and worthy of the place in which it stands. All honor to the noble De Groot! May others imitate him!

Truly yours,

PETER C. BAKER.

[From the Illustrated Christian Weekly.]

CAPT. ALBERT DE GROOT.

Traveling New Yorkers twenty years ago knew Capt. Albert De Groot as one of the most popular and urbane commanders on the North River. Of late years, however, he has been less conspicuously before the public, having long since left the scene of his steamboat labors, to follow the less exciting pursuits of commerce on shore; and fortune has smiled upon him as he deserves. He has grown rich and prosperous, and being without family ties, the liberality of his nature, which otherwise might have been directed in narrower channels, has been devoted to works intended for the general benefit.

His agency in promoting the erection of the immense Vanderbilt Bronzes is fresh in the public mind. The work of art which he yesterday presented to the press of this city again brings his name before the people. The first work was designed as a special tribute to a notably successful man, who, in his earlier years, had given the promoter his aid and friendship. The second, the Statue of Benjamin Franklin, is intended to embody in beautiful and enduring form his appreciation of that substantial kindness which the press invariably exhibited in his behalf during the many years of his career as a steamboat man—kindness and consideration which he has always felt aided him in achieving a success in the battle of life.

At this juncture some slight notice of the antecedents of Capt. De Groot may not be uninteresting to the public. The subject of our sketch, like his friend and patron, Commodore Vanderbilt, is a native of Staten Island. He was a son of Garrett De Groot, an old and respected Staten Islander, and a neighbor and associate of the Vanderbilts. Mr. Cornelius Vanderbilt. who had worked his way up from the command of a periagua, to be a rising steamboat captain, builder and owner, was applied to by his neighbor De Groot to take the young Albert into his service. When the boy called upon the Commodore, to report for duty, the latter demanded,

"What can you do?"

"Almost anything," said he; "Try me, sir."

The Commodore liked the boy's readiness. He said, "I will, Albert. Be a good boy, do right, and you may yet make your mark in the world."

The lad treasured up this counsel, and with the example before him. soon rose from the deck to a command. In time he became master of the Sandusky, the Osceola, the Niagara, and the Reindeer, the two latter in their day the crack boats on the Hudson. In these positions the Captain won golden opinions and substantial success.

His next work was the erection of the Prescott House, in 1857, which in beauty of design, general comfort, and elegance of appointment, was then second to no similar establishment in the country. He introduced the more modern style of ornate steamboat decoration in the steamboat Jenny Lind, which he constructed about the time the Swedish Nightingale came to our shores. From that beginning, dates the floating palaces which now ply upon the inland waters of the United States.

During the war, he built the steamers Resolute and Reliance, two boats which the Government purchased, and which afterward became famous in the naval service. His latest work in ship building was the splendid steamship Jacob H. Vanderbilt, which he named after the Commodore's brother.

Capt. De Groot is still in the prime of life—a hale and hearty man. May his example in beautifying the city and improving its waste places by the erection of works of art, be followed by other citizens of liberal means and generous impulses.

[From the New York Herald.]

JOURNALISM IN FRANKLIN'S TIME.

Benjamin Franklin commenced the publication of the Pennsylvania Gazette, at Philadelphia, in 1739, which was the fourth newspaper enterprise in America at that time. In his prospectus, Franklin announced his purpose to "make a good readable journal," and it soon became apparent that his was to be the leading spirit of journalism, as he was far in advance of his cotemporaries in his ideas of the aims and objects of a public paper. The Gazette consisted of four small pages, and the subscription price was "ten shillings a year." The following advertisement in Franklin's newspaper shows the locale of the Post-office, and speed with which the mail was carried at that early period:

"——, October 27, 1739.

"Notice is hereby given that the Post-office of Philadelphia is now kept at Franklin's, in Market Street, and that Henry Pratt is appointed riding postmaster for all stages between Philadelphia and Newport in Virginia, who sets out about the beginning of each month, and returns in twenty-four days—by whom gentlemen, merchants and others may have their letters carefully conveyed and business faithfully transacted, he having given good security for the same to the Hon. Col. Spotswood, Postmaster-general of all his Majesty's dominions in America."

On the 24th of April, 1704, the first paper printed in the English language in the American Colonies or on the North American continent was issued under the title of the Boston News Letter—a small half sheet printed in *pica* type. It was issued weekly by John Campbell, a Scotchman, at that time engaged as a bookseller and also as postmaster. The leading article in the first issue of the News Letter was a report of the "Queen's Speech in the British Parliament," aside from which the news matter was meagre, consisting merely of a few local articles under the Boston head, one advertisement, some extracts from the London papers, and four paragraphs of marine news. Advertisements in the News Letter were inserted "at reasonable rates, from twopence to five shillings."

In 1721 James Franklin established a newspaper in Boston. The paper was severely critical withal, somewhat hostile to the clergy. Its editor became unpopular, was censured and imprisoned "for scandalous libel." Subsequently, James Franklin was strictly forbidden to issue his paper, the New England Courant, without a "censorium," etc. He evaded this edict by substituting his brother's name for his own. The Courant maintained an existence for three years.

The American Weekly Mercury, published at Philadelphia, in 1722, was the third newspaper printed in the colonies. It was made up of quaint advertisements and short paragraphs.

The first *daily* paper published in the United States was at Philadelphia, in 1795, and was called the Pennsylvania Packet, afterward called the Advertiser.

These were the pioneer attempts at journalism in America, and, as such, are alone worthy of mention. Soon after the advent of the daily newspaper press, the idea of collating and digesting the news became more and more comprehensive, and from the beginning of the present century up to this time, the American newspaper press has grown steadily and rapidly, until it now represents the whole world, and is more mighty than kings and thrones.

New York seems to have been twenty-one years behind Boston in the matter of newspaper enterprise, the first paper having been established in 1725 by William Bradford, under the title of the New York Gazette. The size was about a sheet of foolscap. Eight years after, the New York Weekly Journal was started by John Philip Lengar—the most fearless, if not the most forcible, of the earlier newspaper editors. Lengar was indicted for libeling the Government, was defended by Alexander Hamilton, and acquitted, and received as a public testimonial the freedom of the city and a magnificent gold box. The following extract from the paper of Mr. Lengar, setting forth his ideas of men in public places, is sound doctrine, even applicable to our times:

> "In public affairs it is the duty of young men to be free from personal prejudices; neither ought we to oppose any step that is taking for the good of our country merely because those that are the contrivers and advisers of it are obnoxious to us. There are but too many precedents of this nature, when men have cast the most black colors on the wisest of administrations because those that had the direction of affairs were their enemies in private life; and this ill way of judging may be attended with dangerous consequences to the common weal."

The locality chosen for the site of the Franklin Statue, now popularly known as "Printing-House Square," has grown to be the great center of the metropolitan press, and as fully merits the title as does "Printing-House Square" in London, from whence the name is borrowed. At the present time, it is not difficult to count fifty different newspaper establishments within a stone's throw of the monument, while as many more may be added within a radius of a few blocks of the place. The old brick church edifice destroyed nearly twenty years ago to give place to the Times building, had grouped around it some of the first newspaper establishments of the day, while Spruce and Nassau Streets were famous in connection with printing-houses, among which was the time honored "Tract House," still holding its position, and old Daniel Fanshaw's printing-office near by.

[From the Illustrated Christian Weekly.]

PRINTING-HOUSE SQUARE AS IT WAS.

In the earlier days of Printing-House Square, New York City, before the name of the square had been thought of, no printing was done on the premises. The American Tract Society was the pioneer, and the next the New York Observer. When the Tract Society was formed in 1825, the ground on which its beautiful house now stands was occupied by a miserable old wooden tavern, and its surroundings on Nassau and Spruce Streets were in keeping with it. Spruce Street was a narrow lane, but soon after was widened thirty feet. On its northeast corner, the Sun, the first daily penny paper, and the Plebeian, were printed before the Tribune building was erected.

Directly opposite the Tract House on Nassau Street, where the Times office now is, was an old one-story wooden lecture-room, and on Beekman Street was the Brick Church, between which was a graveyard with many brown and broken headstones.

From the upper stories of the Tract House, between the church and the lecture-room, there was a delightful outlook across the Park. In 1826, the New York Observer occupied the third story of the building. One afternoon, after a beautiful shower, when the declining sun was shining with all its brilliancy through the opening leaves and upon the green grass of the Park, as a number of gentlemen were admiring the view, Professor Morse graphically remarked, "The people who occupy this house have a fine prospect beyond the grave!"

After a few years, the wooden lecture-room gave place to a large brick chapel, which stood till 1856, when it was demolished with the Brick Church itself, and the beautiful Times Building was erected, covering the whole area.

The improvement thus commenced by the Tract Society, in 1825, has since been steadily going on. New buildings have been erected. Spruce Street has been almost wholly built up, and Nassau Street rebuilt far down below Beekman and Ann Streets. The printing has been extended, till, in addition to all the book printing, several of the leading secular and religious journals are located upon, and send out their immense daily and weekly issues from, Printing-House Square.

[From the Illustrated Police News, January 25, 1872.]

ASSAULT ON THE STATUE.

(BEFORE THE UNVEILING.)

An exciting scene occurred in Printing-House Square, New York, at half-past 12 o'clock on the 15th January. A person, supposed to be crazy, rushed down Chatham Street with a huge knife in his hand, and, climbing upon the large pedestal on which the Statue of Franklin is placed, proceeded to tear the flag off and to hack the Statue with the knife.

A large crowd gathered around, and various means were resorted to in order to get the man down. The police rushed to the place and endeavored to reach the man with their clubs, but he was too quick. Stones, sticks, missiles and various things were hurled at the man, without any effect.

He continued for several minutes cutting and tearing the flag, till at last his foot slipped and he fell to the ground. The police seized him, but he fought terribly, and the police had to use their clubs, which excited the wrath of the crowd to such a degree that the police stopped their clubbing for fear the crowd would attack them. He was taken to the station-house, followed by a large crowd.

He gave his name as Diedrich Barr, thirty-seven years of age, of German birth, and a sailor by occupation. He stated that he was passing by and desired to know who was concealed beneath the covering of the flag, and that he meant no harm.

He laughed heartily over the matter, being rather slightly intoxicated and full of mischief. He was dressed in a black suit, very neatly, with a slouched hat.

www.ingramcontent.com/pod-product-compliance
Lightning Source LLC
Chambersburg PA
CBHW032151010726
47493CB00008BA/2659

* 9 7 8 3 3 3 7 2 5 2 7 2 4 *